# Bildliche Redewendungen Englisch

Mit Anwendungsbeispielen, Übersetzungen und Register

Von

DAPHNE M. GULLAND

LANGENSCHEIDT

BERLIN · MÜNCHEN · WIEN · ZÜRICH · NEW YORK

Illustrationen: Achim Theil


| | | | | | | |
|---|---|---|---|---|---|---|
| *Auflage:* | *5.* | *4.* | *3.* | *2.* | *1.* | *Letzte Zahlen* |
| *Jahr:* | *2000* | *1999* | *98* | *97* | *96* | *maßgeblich* |





*Druck: Druckhaus Langenscheidt KG, Berlin-Schöneberg*

*Printed in Germany · ISBN 3-468-43345-X*

# Vorwort

Jeder Muttersprachler gebraucht sie täglich, und in allen englischsprachigen Zeitungen und Büchern findet man sie laufend: die bildlichen Redewendungen oder "similes", wie sie im Englischen heißen, die eine Sprache erst anschaulich und lebendig machen. Sie werden besonders gern und häufig benutzt, um zwei unterschiedliche Gegenstände oder Begriffe miteinander zu vergleichen, damit sie uns plastischer vor Augen stehen.

Woran erkennt man die bildlichen Vergleiche im Englischen? Sie können entweder mit *as (as slippery as an eel, as free as a bird, as cross as a bear with a sore head, fit as a flee)* oder aber mit *like* gebildet werden (z.B.: *to cling like a limpet, to sell like hot cakes, to laugh like a jelly, to look like the back end of a tram etc.*).

Sie können aber auch in verkürzter Form auftreten, indem sie – ohne *as* – als Adjektive erscheinen, wie z. B. *dust-dry, razor-sharp, ice-cold, drainpipe-thin, dirt-cheap, sky-high, sure-fire etc.* Oder aber *like* wird an das Substantiv angehängt wie in *bird-like, waif-like, child-like* oder *dream-like.*

Manche vergleichende bildliche Redewendungen sind *"as easy as ABC"* und verstehen sich – auch für den deutschen Benutzer – von selbst, wie z.B. *as free as a bird* oder auch *as white as snow*. Wenn sie dagegen bereits zu idiomatischen Wendungen geworden sind, ist es schon wesentlich schwieriger, ihren Sinn zu entschlüsseln. Beispiele hierfür wären: *as right as rain, as sure as eggs is eggs* und *as mad as a March Hare.*

Daphne Gulland hat nun in dem vorliegenden Buch sowohl bekannte "similes" wie *as busy as a bee* als auch moderne bildliche Prägungen wie *to repeat like a cracked record* zusammengetragen und in 29 Kapitel unterteilt. Jeder bildliche Vergleich wird – sofern möglich – wörtlich ins Deutsche übertragen oder aber sinngemäß umschrieben. Es folgt ein englisches Anwendungsbeispiel, das den Gebrauch im Kontext veranschaulicht (oft auch mit Quellenangabe). Durch Querverweise wird auf bildliche Redewendungen mit identischer, ähnlicher, aber auch gegensätzlicher Bedeutung hingewiesen. Die zahlreichen humorvollen Illustrationen dienen der bildlichen Veranschaulichung und sorgen zugleich für

Auflockerung. Als sprachliche Quellen dienten namhafte englische Zeitungen, wie *The Daily Mail, The Sunday Times* und *The European,* und Bestsellerromane wie *The Flame Trees of Thika* von Elspeth Huxley, *Hotel Pastis* von Peter Mayle, *Jericho* von Dirk Bogarde, *The Fourth Horseman* von Andrew Nikiforuk, *Every Living Thing* von James Herriot, *Night Shall Overtake Us* von Kate Saunders, *The Shell Seekers* von Rosamunde Pilcher, *Miss Smilla's Feeling For Snow* von Peter Hoeg, und die Bücher von Dean Koontz und Stephen King.

Ein ausführliches Inhaltsverzeichnis und ein differenzierter Index im Anhang ermöglichen gezielten und schnellen Zugriff auf den gesuchten bildlichen Vergleich. Sie runden ein Werk ab, das jedem an der englischen Sprache Interessierten eine praktische und nützliche Hilfe bei der Erweiterung seines Wortschatzes und der Verbesserung seiner Ausdrucksfähigkeit bietet. In diesem Sinne: "Happy simile-seeking!"

# Inhaltsverzeichnis

# 1. Colours – *Farben*

## RED

– **like painting a dead man's face red** – als ob man Tatsachen verschleiern würde.

Giving the impression that Russia is not interested in re-establishing its influence in Georgia is **like painting a dead man's face red**.

– **to be like a red rag to a bull (to someone)** – (auf jemanden) wie ein rotes Tuch wirken.

It was **like a red rag to a bull** each time old Mrs Jones saw the children playing tennis on the road alongside her garden. The tennis balls always ended up amongst her flowers.

– **tomato-red hair** – feuerrotes Haar.

"Have you seen Jane's boyfriend? He's got **tomato-red hair**."

– **as red as a tomato/beetroot** – rot wie eine Tomate.

"When Sophie noticed that she was wearing her jumper inside out she went **as red as a beetroot**."

– **as red as a turkey-cock** – puterrot.

"You should have seen him in front of all those girls! He turned **as red as a turkey-cock**."

– **as red as a lobster** – rot wie ein Krebs, krebsrot.

The young man lay too long in the hot sun and his back was **as red as a lobster**.

– **blood-red** – blutrot.

The morning of Friday, April 13th dawned **blood-red**. (Winter by Len Deighton, 1987. cf. ruby-red.)

– **as red as fire** – feuerrot.

The sea rippled **as red as fire** as we rowed towards the setting sun.

– **to be red hot** – heißlaufen.

When the controversial film came to an end, the BBC's telephone was **red hot** with calls from viewers protesting about its violence. cf. *the idiom*: a red hot socialist.

– **as red as a rose** – rot wie eine Rose, rosenrot.

O my Luve's **like a red, red rose**
That's newly sprung in June:
O my Luve's **like the melody**
That's sweetly played in tune.

(A Red, Red Rose by Robert Burns, 1759–1796.)

## PINK

– **flamingo-pink** – knallrosa.

"Our neighbour really has no taste. Her **flamingo-pink** curtains clash terribly with her **lime-green** carpet".

## BLUE

– **to come like a bolt from the blue/like a lightning bolt from the blue** – wie ein Blitz aus heiterem Himmel kommen.

The news that the village post office would have to close **came like a bolt from the blue**.

When our daughter, Hayley, suddenly appeared on our doorstep and told us she was not going back to university, it was **like a lightning bolt from the blue**.

## GREEN

– **to be as green as grass** – noch naß hinter den Ohren/unreif/unerfahren sein.

"You cannot expect Silvia to do business with such people. She is only nineteen and **as green as grass**."

– **to be as green as old school dinners** – *etwa:* grün vor Neid sein.

"When Emma hears that I've won a ticket to the Pink Floyd pop concert she'll be **as green as old school dinners**!" NB. *the idiom:* to be green with envy.

– **not as green as one is cabbage-looking** – nicht so dumm, wie man aussieht.

"I don't believe this picture here is a real Picasso. I'm not **as green as I'm cabbage-looking**."

– **pea-green** – lindgrün, erbsengrün.

Paul was the proud owner of a new **pea-green** boat with white sails. cf. emerald green; lime-green.

## YELLOW

– **yellow as gold** – so gelb wie Gold, goldgelb.

Her lips were red, her looks were free,
Her **locks were yellow as gold**:
Her **skin was as white as leprosy**,
The Nightmare Life-in-Death was she,
Who thicks man's blood with cold.

(The Rime of the Ancient Mariner by Samuel Taylor Coleridge, 1772–1834, from part III.)

– **canary-yellow** – kanariengelb, knallgelb.

The Queen Mother wore a **canary-yellow** coat and matching hat at the ceremony to open the new university.

## WHITE

– **to be like a whited sepulchre** – *etwa:* Außen hui, innen pfui; der Schein trügt; wie eine hohle Fassade.

"I wouldn't put my money into that bank, if I were you. It is **like a whited sepulchre** and there is a rumour that the bank manager is involved in fraud."

– **as white as a lily/lily-white** – weiß wie eine Lilie.

Then Aragorn stooped and **looked** in her face, and it was indeed **white as a lily, cold as frost, and hard as graven stone**. (The Lord of the Rings by J. R. R. Tolkien, 1955.) NB. whiter than white.

– **as white as snow/snow-white** – weiß wie Schnee, schneeweiß.

The Queen said to herself, "Oh, what I would give to have a child **as white as snow, as red as blood** and **as black as ebony**!" (Snow White and the Seven Dwarfs by Jakob (1785–1863) and Wilhelm Grimm (1786–1859).)

The early days of the Chelsea Flower Show were like a fashion parade of very dressed-up society ladies, wearing **snow-white** gloves and giant toadstool hats. (Carol Thatcher, daughter of Britain's former Prime Minister, Daily Mail, 23.7.1994.) cf. skin as soft as silk; skin like a peach/like a rhinoceros; as white as milk; milk-white; to look as white as a ghost/a sheet. *A variation:* **as white as a dove/chalk**.

## BLACK

– **as black as soot/as black as pitch/as black as tar/as black as coal/ as black as ebony** – pechschwarz, rabenschwarz.

Andrew's shoes were **as black as soot** after his walk in the muddy wood.

After rolling about in the mud the dog was **as black as coal**.

The cellar walls of the ancient castle were **as black as tar**.

cf. raven-black; as black as Hades/hell/thunder.

– **as black as the ace of spades** – schwarz wie Teer, schmutzig.

The tins of canned fruit were old and badly dented and when we opened them the fruit inside was **as black as the ace of spades**.

– **like a pot calling a kettle black** – *etwa:* Wer im Glashaus sitzt, sollte nicht mit Steinen werfen.

"You needn't tell me that my bedroom is in a terrible mess, dear sister. Just look at yours! It's **like the pot calling the kettle black**."

– **not as black as one is painted** – nicht so schlecht wie sein Ruf.

"Brian did all the shopping for the sick old woman. He's not **as black as he is painted**."

– **like the Black Hole of Calcutta** – *etwa:* sehr heiß, beengt und unbequem.

"This discotheque is far too crowded. Let's get out of here. It's **like the Black Hole of Calcutta**."

## BROWN

– **to be as brown as a berry** – kaffeebraun, braungebrannt sein.

The little girl was **as brown as a berry** after her day in Bournemouth. cf. as brown as a walnut.

– **chocolate-brown** – schokoladenbraun.

Vincent's **chocolate-brown** poodle won first prize at the dog-show.

## GREY

– **steel-grey** – stahlgrau.

Physically, Vince has aged well. His **steel-grey** hair is probably the only sign of his 57 years. (Lester Middlehurst writing about the pop singer Vince Hill, Daily Mail, 12.1.1995.)

## PAINT

– **like painting the Forth Bridge** – *etwa:* wie eine nie enden wollende Arbeit.

"Writing a dictionary is **like painting the Forth Bridge** – no sooner have you finished than it's time to start again!" (Keith Waterhouse, Daily Mail, 2.9.1993.)

like being on another planet

– **as interesting as watching paint dry** – stinklangweilig.

The conference went on and on for hours on end and was **as interesting as watching paint dry**.

## 2. Elements – *Elemente*

### AIR

– **as free as the air** – frei und unbeschwert.

"Now that I have passed my exams, I feel **as free as the air** and can do whatever I like." cf. as free as the wind; as free as a bird.

– **as light as air** – 1. leicht wie eine Feder, federleicht; 2. ohne Substanz, ohne geistigen Tiefgang.

Her new shoes carried her **as light as air** over the dance floor.

The argument was **as light as air**. It had no impact whatsoever. cf. as light as a feather.

– **like a lot of hot air** – nichts als leeres Geschwätz.

"Don't take any notice of William's threats. They are **like a lot of hot air** and nothing to worry about."

– **to come/seem like a breath of fresh air** – wie eine frische Brise kommen/erscheinen.

Fergie was **like a breath of fresh air** to Diana ... but she was more than a breath of fresh air. She was the wind of change. (Behind Palace Doors by Nigel Dempster and Peter Evans, 1993.)

## PLANET

– **like being on another planet** – als ob man auf einem anderen Stern wäre.

To the Londoners, walking amongst the spluttering mudholes and erupting geysers of the National Park was **like being on another planet**.

## EARTH

– **to look like nothing on earth** – wie eine Schreckschraube aussehen; schrecklich aussehen.

"You **look like nothing on earth** with that terrible hat on!" cf. to look like a dog's dinner.

– **like falling off the end of the earth** – als ob man ins Bodenlose fällt/den Boden unter den Füßen verliert.

In Corsica you can get a good three-course meal for under £ 12 anywhere. But, if you put one step off the set menu, **it's like falling off the end of the earth**, it's so expensive! (Diana Hutchinson, Daily Mail, 15.10.1994.)

## HILLS

– **as old as the hills** – steinalt/uralt.

"That song you are singing is **as old as the hills**. Did you learn it at school?" cf. as old as Adam, as old as Methuselah. *A variation:* **as old as time/an oak tree**.

## WATER

– **like water on a hot stone** – wie ein Tropfen auf den heißen Stein.

"It's no good telling John off for getting bad marks at school. That's **like water on a hot stone**."

– **to be like water down the drain** – den Bach hinuntergehen, unwiederbringlich verloren sein.

"Don't buy her that necklace. She's got so many already and it would be **like water down the drain**."

– **as weak as water/dishwater/to taste like water** – dünn wie Spülwasser (schmecken).

The young man hadn't put enough tea-bags into the pot and the tea was **as weak as water**.

– **as dull as ditch water** – überaus langweilig/stinklangweilig.

"I'm trying very hard to enjoy my library book but it is **as dull as ditch water**."

"Must you always buy yourself such **dull-as-ditch-water** suits?"

– **to disappear like water on sand** – wie vom Erdboden verschluckt sein.

If only we could remember our dreams better, but they just **disappear like water on sand**.

As soon as the illegal immigrants get across the border, they **disappear like water on sand**.

*Variations:* **to disappear like coals into a furnace; to disappear like a conjurer's rabbit**.

– **champagne is flowing like water** – Champagner fließt in Strömen.

We could tell that our hosts were terribly rich. We were offered only the very best food and the **champagne was flowing like water**. cf. like confetti.

## POND

– **as calm as a millpond/like a millpond** – spiegelglatt, ruhig.

"I needn't have worried about being seasick. The English Channel was **as calm as a millpond**."

## MUD

– **as clear as mud** – völlig unklar, undurchsichtig.

"Helen, you really must write down your school timetable for me again. This one is **as clear as mud**." cf. *the opposite:* as clear as crystal.

## MUCK

– **to be as common as muck** – sehr schlechte Manieren haben; gewöhnlich und primitiv sein.

"For goodness sake, don't talk to her. She's **as common as muck**."

## DIRT

– **dirt cheap** – spottbillig.

"I got this jumper **dirt cheap** at the market but now I'm home I can see there's a hole in it."

– **as poor as dirt/dirt-poor** – bettelarm.

In New Delhi, tetracycline capsules, the plague preventative medicine, were available on the black market for twice the normal price – meaning the **dirt-poor** will have to find 2 to be sure of one week's supply. (Brian Vine, Daily Mail, 30.9.1994.)

– **to treat someone like dirt/like a piece of dirt** – jemanden wie den letzten Dreck behandeln.

"I'm not at all surprised that Jane doesn't want to work as a maid in Honeymead House anymore. That old crosspatch **treated her like dirt**." cf. to treat like a leper/a pariah/a toe-rag/an animal/a dog/whipped dogs; *and the opposite:* to treat like a king; to treat like a celebrity; to treat something like gold.

## DUST

– **as dry as dust/dust-dry** – knochentrocken; staubtrocken; stinklangweilig.

You can lay turf at any time of year, provided that the soil is neither frozen hard, squelching with mud or **dust-dry**. (Alan Titchmarsh, Daily Mail, 1.10.1994.)

The Professor made the lecture on church law in the 19th century sound **as dry as dust** and the students got rather restless.

## STONE

– **to fall/sink like a stone** – wie ein Stein fallen/versinken.

A skydiver **fell like a stone** and broke both his legs after losing control of his parachute.

Three fishermen had to jump for their lives as their boat **sank like a stone** into the stormy waters. cf. sink like a brick; sink like lead.

– **the temperature drops like a stone** – die Temperatur sinkt rapide.

The weather forecaster looked rather sadly at his audience and announced that the **temperature** the next day **would drop like a stone**.

– **as immobile as stone** – versteinert; ausdruckslos; unbewegt.

"The old woman begged the official to help her but his **face** remained **as immobile as stone**." cf. as still/motionless as a statue; to set one's face like flint/granite. NB. *the adjective:* stony-silent.

**– stone cold/as cold as stone** – kalt wie Stein, eiskalt.

"I'm afraid Bill's telephone call interrupted my lunch and now it is **stone cold**".

Louisa's pet mouse was lying motionless and **as cold as stone** on the floor of its cage, but luckily it made a speedy recovery when placed near the warm radiator.

**– stone dead/as dead as stone/stones** – mausetot.

The age of the gentleman is in its last dying moments – if not **stone dead** already – and we need to revive it. (Allan Massie, Daily Mail, 7.10.1994.)

In the science fiction film we saw all the monsters fighting each other, and quite a few of them ended up **as dead as stones**.
cf. as dead as a door-nail/as a tent-peg/as Queen Anne. *Variations:* **as dead as a herring/a shotten herring/a mouse/a mutton**.

**– like a stone in the shoe** – *etwa:* ein Dorn im Auge.

like a stone in the shoe

"I'll be so glad when that unpleasant teacher has left our school", the headmaster sighed. "He's **like a stone in the shoe**." cf. like a thorn in one's flesh.

– **as hard as the nether millstone** – hart wie Stein; hartherzig, gefühllos.

"That young man doesn't care at all that his widowed mother is poor and lonely. He's **as hard as the nether millstone**." cf. like a millstone round one's neck; as hard/tough as nails; as hard as stone/as rock. NB. *the idiom:* stone-hearted.

## GRAVEL

– **a voice like gravel** – eine Stimme wie ein Reibeisen.

The American singer Lee Marvin had **a voice like gravel** but everyone loved his song "Wandering Star". cf. a voice like sandpaper/like an angel; a voice as cold as steel/as smooth as syrup/as soft as a prayer.

## MARBLE

– **as cold as marble** – kalt wie eine Hundeschnauze, gleichgültig und gefühlskalt.

"My son's teacher is **as cold as marble**. He doesn't seem to care if Mark gets upset about something." cf. as cold as steel; as cold as ice; as cold as charity; as cold as a paddock.

## ROCK

– **as steady as a rock** – wie ein Fels in der Brandung; wie festgenagelt.

"The marksman aimed his gun **as steady as a rock** at his target and shot a bull's eye."

– **as hard as rock/as stone** – hart wie Stein, steinhart.

"The sweet was **as hard as rock** and the child had to spit it out." cf. food hard/tough as old boots.

## FIRE

**– as hot as fire** – feurig; heiß wie Feuer.

"He soon noticed that her **passion was as hot as fire**." cf. as hot as a furnace/an oven; as hot as a griddle; volcano-like.

**– as quick as fire/quick-fire; quick-fire gags, jokes,** etc. – wie aus der Pistole geschossen.

The Lion King is a very funny film. The script is the wittiest yet written for a Disney cartoon, full of wisecracks and **quick-fire gags** shared out liberally among a terrific cast. (Jack Tinker, Daily Mail, 7.10.1994.)

**– as sure as fire/sure-fire** – todsicher, zuverlässig.

All Rosamund Pilcher's books are **sure-fire best-sellers**.

Does anyone have a **sure-fire solution** to moles digging up one's lawn?

## WILDFIRE/BUSH-FIRE

**– to spread like wildfire/like a bush-fire** – sich wie ein Buschfeuer ausbreiten.

When the doctor and the nurse were seen kissing each other outside the operating theatre, the **news spread like wildfire** around the hospital.

Joy Adamson betrayed husbands, mistreated servants, quarrelled with officials and went through lovers **like a bush-fire**. (Daily Mail, 30.8.1992.)

cf. like a whirlwind; to spread like a wild sex rumour/a contagion/a virus/a rash/like fungus.

## SOOT/COAL/PITCH

**– as easy as juggling with soot** – sehr schwierig, fast aussichtslos.

"Trying to find my wife in Oxford Street will be **as easy as juggling with soot**." cf. as easy as nailing jelly to the wall.

– **pitch dark/as dark as pitch** – schwarz/dunkel wie die Nacht; stockduster.

Suddenly the cellar light went out and it was **pitch dark**. cf. as dark as night. *Pitch dark is used more than as dark as pitch.*

– **like walking on hot coals** – als ob man auf heißen Kohlen geht.

She was the only girl in a class full of boys. Being at that school was **like walking on hot coals for her**. cf. like a cat on hot bricks.

## VOLCANO

– **like sitting/picnicking/walking on a volcano** – wie ein Tanz auf dem Vulkan. *An American simile.*

"Working under Kelvin MacKenzie, former Editor of the Sun was said to be **like picnicking on a volcano**. Pleasant, provided you leave before it blows up." (Daily Mail, 22.1.1994.)

like sitting on a volcano

– **volcano-like/like a volcano waiting to erupt** – wie ein schlummernder Vulkan/Vulkan vor dem Ausbruch.

"Whenever I see you, you make me feel totally erotic and **volcano-like**. I love you desperately." Silvia read the letter from her admirer several times and smiled wickedly to herself.

In the play "The Browning Version" Greta Scacchi plays Laura, a deeply frustrated wife. Her sexuality is repressed **like a volcano waiting to erupt**. (Angela Levin, Daily Mail, 7.10.1994.)

cf. passion as hot as fire.

## OIL

– **like pouring oil on the flames** – als ob man Öl ins Feuer gießt.

Arming the civilians would be **like pouring oil on the flames**. NB. *the idiom:* to pour oil on troubled waters.

## STEEL

– **as cold as steel** – kalt wie Eis/eine Hundeschnauze.

The stranger looked unfriendly and his **voice** was **as cold as steel**. cf. a voice as smooth as syrup; a voice like a little bell/an angel; as cold as marble/ice/as cold as charity; steel-grey.

– **as true as steel** – verläßlich und beständig wie Stahl.

"Our love is **as true as steel**", Peter whispered in his girlfriend's ear, making her giggle in delight.

– **to have a mind like a steel trap** – eine schnelle Auffassungsgabe haben/sich leicht ein bestimmtes Wissen aneignen.

"It's no wonder he was chosen to be editor of the new encyclopaedia. He has a **mind like a steel trap**."

## LEAD

– **as heavy as lead/to feel like lead** – schwer wie Blei, sich schwer wie Blei fühlen/wie Blei in den Gliedern liegen.

On hearing the news that she was no longer needed at the hospital her heart was **as heavy as lead**.

"We had to walk up so many steep hills and now my **feet feel like lead**!"

After standing the whole day at the counter, the shopkeeper's **legs felt like lead**. *A variation:* **as heavy as a brick.**

– **to sink like lead** – wie Blei/ein Stein versinken/untergehen.

The selfsame moment I could pray;
And from my neck so free
The Albatross fell off, and **sank**
**Like lead into the sea.**

(The Rime of the Ancient Mariner by Samuel Taylor Coleridge, 1772–1834, from part IV.) cf. to sink like a stone/a brick.

– **words fall like lead** – Worte schlagen wie ein Blitz ein/haben eine rasche, intensive Wirkung.

The Minister's **words fell like lead** and a long silence followed. No one knew quite what to say. cf. to go down like a lead balloon.

## BRASS

– **as bold as brass** – frech wie Rotze, unverschämt.

"Kevin asked me what my income was the first time we met. That man is **as bold as brass**." NB. *the idiom:* a brass neck – *someone who is very impudent*; *and* brass-necked cheek.

## FLINT

– **to set ones face like flint** – unnachgiebig wie Stein, steinhart sein.

The general has **set his face like flint** against sending any more soldiers into that faraway country.

## SLATE

– **as hard/cold as slate** – hart und kalt wie ein Stein; rauh.

It wasn't such a good idea to go sailing today. The sea was **as hard and cold as slate** and made us shiver.

## MAGNET

– **to be drawn to someone/something like a magnet/like iron filings to a magnet/like filings magnetised** – von jemandem/etwas angezogen werden wie von einem Magnet.

Suzanna had such an attractive face, and her **ruby-red**, slightly pouting lips **drew Simon to her like a magnet**. How he longed to kiss her!

The horse could not do without Manhattan. It **drew** him **like a magnet, like a vacuum**, like oats, or a mare, or an open, never-ending, tree-lined road. (Winter's Tale by Mark Helprin, 1983.)

In all the soap opera scrapes and shenanigans to which the younger Royals have been **attracted like iron filings to a magnet** in recent years, only one leading figure comes out of it all completely unscathed, together with her Mum, and that is the head of the House of Windsor herself. (Keith Waterhouse, Daily Mail, 24.10.1994.)

*Variations:* a business/a film star/a restaurant, etc. **attracts publicity like iron filings to a magnet**.

At the sergeant's command, the soldiers promptly fell into line, **like filings magnetised**. cf. to draw like bees to a honey pot.

## QUICKSILVER

– **quicksilver mood, reaction, production,** etc. – überaus sprunghafte/wechselhafte/lebhafte Stimmung, Reaktion, Produktion etc.

The artist's **quicksilver mood** left us speechless.

Peter Hall's **quicksilver production** of Hamlet is superbly detailed, but also athletic and agile. Hall knows, as Shakespeare knew, that you must seize your audience's attention at once. (John Peter, The Sunday Times, The Culture, 13.11.1994.)

# 3. Weather – *Wetter*

## WEATHER

– **as changeable as the weather** – wechselhaft/sprunghaft wie das Wetter.

"You can't rely on her, she is **as changeable as the weather**."

– **to change/spin like a weather-cock** – sich drehen wie eine Wetterfahne; seine Fahne nach dem Wind drehen; ein Wendehals sein.

Should not the Established Church give a moral lead on whether Prince Charles should divorce, re-marry and reign, instead of **spinning like a weather-cock** in a wind of change? (Daily Mail Comment, 24.10.1994.)

sky-high

## SKY

– **sky-high** – turmhoch/himmelhoch.

"You shouldn't drink so much coffee, Granny. All that caffeine will send your blood pressure **sky-high**."

The price of antique Steiff toys has shot **sky-high**. cf. to shoot like a rocket.

– **as limitless as the sky** – grenzenlos/unendlich wie der Himmel/das Universum; turmhoch.

"If you take over this business, your ventures will be **as limitless as the sky**."

## RAIN

– **to be/feel as right as rain** – sich pudelwohl fühlen, kerngesund sein; total in Ordnung sein.

"That medicine from the doctor is very good. You will soon **feel as right as rain**."

The old lady was shocked when her chest of drawers fell apart but her son said: "Don't worry. I'll hammer a few nails into it and then it will be **as right as rain**." cf. as right as ninepence. *Variation:* **as right as a trivet**.

## SNOW

– **as pure as the driven snow** – rein wie ein Engel, die reine Unschuld.

The eloquent lawyer found it easy to persuade the jury that the prisoner in the dock was **as pure as the driven snow**.

## SLUSH

– **as pure as the driven slush** – unrein; ein schlechter Charakter.

"Don't be deceived by that handsome young man. He is **as pure as the driven slush**."

## SNOWBALL

- **to have as much chance of getting something as a snowball in hell** – absolut keine Chance/null Chancen haben.

"Lazy Tom has as much chance of getting into university **as a snowball in hell**." NB. Hell will freeze over before that happens.

## SNOW-STORM

- **as likely as a snow-storm in Karachi/like snow in Rome** – so wahrscheinlich wie Schnee in Rom/ein Schneesturm in Karachi.

"I think it would be **like snow in Rome**, having a republican Lord Mayor in New York", the politician told the reporter.

## ICE

- **as cold as ice/ice-cold** – eiskalt, hundekalt.

We had forgotten our umbrellas and **ice-cold** raindrops fell down on us.

After our long walk by the sea my hands and feet were **as cold as ice**. cf. as cold as marble; as cold as steel; as cold as charity.

- **as independent as a hog on ice** – unabhängig wie ein Kleinkind; im Gegensatz zur Realität nach eigener Überzeugung selbständig und unabhängig.

"Did I hear you say that Roger wants to go on a six-week camping trip around Europe? That's a laugh! He's **as independent as a hog on ice**!"

## CLOUD

- **to hang over someone/something like a cloud/a dark cloud** – wie eine dunkle Wolke über jemandem/etwas hängen.

There is a growing wave of lawlessness in South Africa. **Crime and violence hang like a dark cloud over our land**. (President F. W. de Klerk, Daily Mail, 30.1.1993.) cf. hang over someone like an overdue debt; like the sword of Damocles hanging over one. *A variation:* **to hover over someone like a poison cloud**.

to hang over s.o. like a dark cloud

## WIND

– **to run like the wind** – laufen wie ein geölter Blitz.

"The boy **ran like the wind** in the school race and won the first prize." cf. to run like lightning; to run like a hare.

– **as free as the wind** – frei und ungebunden.

With her five children all safely back at boarding school, the mother felt **as free as the wind**. cf. as free as the air/as a bird.

– **like whistling in the wind** – als ob man in den Wind redet.

"It's **like whistling in the wind** talking to Christopher about his friends."

– **like spitting into the wind** – als ob man gegen taube Ohren redet/gegen den Wind spuckt/redet.

Trying to get the children to do their homework without listening to their music in the background is **like spitting into the wind**.

– **like tilting at windmills** – als ob man gegen Windmühlen ankämpft.

“Why do you always attack private schools, Joshua? There are hardly any private schools left in London. It’s **like tilting at windmills**.”

## BREEZE

– **like a breeze** – spielerisch, ohne Anstrengung, wie im Vorübergehen. *An American simile.*

“Marion passed all her university exams **like a breeze**.”

## STORM

– **like the calm before the storm** – wie die Ruhe vor dem Sturm.

“It’s suddenly so quiet. Where have all the rioters gone? It’s **like the calm before the storm**.”

## TORNADO/WHIRLWIND

– **like a tornado/whirlwind** – wie ein Wirbelwind.

Everything was in a mess after the long summer holiday but after the mother had blown through the house **like a tornado** it was soon all spick and span again.

David Niven, according to his biographer, went through the female population of Hollywood **like a whirlwind**. (William Cash, Daily Mail, 14.4.1994.) cf. go through lovers like a bush-fire.

## HURRICANE

– **like a hurricane** – wie ein Wirbelsturm.

The infection went through the little boy’s body **like a hurricane**.

“This classroom looks **like it’s been hit by a hurricane**!” the teacher sternly reproached his pupils. “Tidy it up immediately.”

## THUNDER

- **as black as thunder/a face like thunder** – finster wie die Nacht/ein finsteres Gesicht.

"When I stood up to the bully, his face went **as black as thunder**."

"Mr Philpot stormed out of the auction hall with a **face like thunder**, after failing to buy the Greek vase."

- **a noise like thunder/the noise of gunfire,** etc. **comes like thunder** – ein Mordslärm/die Schüsse klangen wie Donnerschläge.

Whilst we were having our breakfast we suddenly heard **a noise like thunder**. Later we found out a car bomb had exploded.

The stillness of the night was rudely interrupted by the noise of gunfire which **came like thunder**.

## LIGHTNING

- **as quick as lightning/as quick as a flash/like lightning/lightning-like/like greased lightning/like a streak of lightning/lightning-fast** – wie ein geölter Blitz, blitzschnell.

Emma, an 18-month-old leopard is capable of running down an intruder at 60 mph without breaking stride. "She's incredibly powerful and **runs like lightning**. That is why she's so dangerous," her owner said to Bill Mouland, Daily Mail, 8.12.1993.

My grandfather gave us his old Ford and in the end **we got it going like greased lightning**.

Trams negotiate the streets of Vienna and Graz at an average speed of ten miles an hour, but this is **lightning-like** progress compared with the daily snarl-ups in London, Paris or Rome. (Xenophobe's Guide to the Austrians by Louis James, 1994.)

Mr Gilbert dropped some money by mistake and **quick as a flash**, the beggar children scooped up the coins and ran off.

E-mail is a **lightning-fast** communications system. Type a message on your computer, connect to the telephone line by a modem, fill in the recipient's mailbox address, and simply press "send". (Christopher Lloyd, Sunday Times, 20.11.1994.) cf. to run like the wind/like a hare. *Variations:* **as quick as thought/a snake**.

## 4. Time – *Zeit*

### TIME

- **like going back/travelling back** forty **years in time/like being plucked back in time** – als ob die Zeit vor vierzig Jahren stehengeblieben/die Uhr um vierzig Jahre zurückgedreht worden ist.

Whenever I visit my grandparents in their little cottage it is **like going back fifty years in time**.

### CLOCK

- **as calm as a clock** – vollkommen ruhig und gelassen.

Mervyn had learnt his Latin so well that he went into the examination room **as calm as a clock**. cf. as calm as a millpond.

- **to go/run like clockwork** – laufen wie am Schnürchen/wie geschmiert; sein Leben bis ins kleinste regeln.

Brian Stimpson **runs his life and his school like clockwork** until he misses his train on his way to chair the Headmasters conference. (The Good Book Guide, October, 1993, reviewing the film Clockwise by Michael Frayn.) cf. go like a charm/dream. *A variation:* **to run like a well-oiled watch**.

### METRONOME

- **to wag/flick like a metronome** – wie ein Metronom hin- und herpendeln.

Rex was so happy to see us again that his **tail wagged like a metronome**.

- **as regular as clockwork/as regular as the clock** – regelmäßig wie ein Uhrwerk; tagein, tagaus.

Sadly, Mr Jones lost his job, but he still caught the train every morning **as regular as clockwork** so that his wife would not suspect anything.

## DAY

– **as open as the day** – wie ein offenes Buch.

"I just can't believe she stole that money. She's **as open as the day**." cf. like an open book; *and the opposite:* to close up like a clam, as close as an oyster.

– **as honest as the day is long** – absolut ehrlich.

I'm **as honest as the day is long**, the longer the daylight, the less I do wrong. (From the song "Shut Up" by Madness, 1981.)

"It was never my intention that we should get involved in anything remotely fraudulent. My aunts are **as honest as the day is long**." (John Herrod talking about his two aunts who are being hunted by the police in Britain and in Ireland. Daily Mail, 26. 7. 1993.)

– **as bright as day** – gleißend hell wie der Tag; taghell.

A glittering light poured out from the door-way on to the stairs, and made everything **as bright as day**. (Felidae by Akif Pirincci, 1989.)

## DAY AND NIGHT

– **as certain as night follows day** – so sicher wie das Amen in der Kirche/todsicher.

"**As certain as night follows day**, she will look after her parents if they become ill." cf. as sure as eggs is eggs.

– **like day and night** – ein Unterschied/unterschiedlich wie Tag und Nacht.

"Crossing the border into Mexico, one can't help noticing that San Diego and Tijuana are **like day and night**." cf. like chalk and cheese.

## NIGHT

– **as dark as night/as the night** – dunkel wie die Nacht.

"The sun was shining beautifully outside but it was **as dark as night** in the tunnel." cf. pitch dark/as dark as pitch.

– **as black as night** – in den schwärzesten Farben.

"Writers know that art, like life, should be a mixture of light and shade. Too many modern television dramatists think that their scripts should be **as black as night**." (Roy Hattersley, Daily Mail, 30. 8. 1994.)

– **like ships in the night/like ships that pass in the night** – *etwa:* flüchtige Begegnung/Bekanntschaft.

"It's such a pity that you're emigrating to New Zealand just when we've met. We are **like ships in the night**."

## TOMORROW

– **like there's no tomorrow/like there was no tomorrow** – als ob morgen die Welt untergehen würde/als ob es morgen nichts mehr geben würde.

The little girl is stuffing herself with chocolate **like there's no tomorrow**.

The tramp was pouring drink into himself **like there was no tomorrow**.

## WEEK-END

– **to look like a wet week-end** – völlig miserabel aussehen.

"You **look like a wet week-end**. Did your boy-friend drop you?"

## HOUR

– **a figure like an hourglass** – eine Wespentaille.

"Pauline Prescott, wife of Labour's new deputy leader, is very glamorous, with an **hourglass figure** and long legs, immaculate hair and make-up." (Geoffrey Levy, Daily Mail, 22. 7. 1994.)

an hourglass figure

## 5. Life and Death – *Leben und Tod*

### LIFE

– **as large as life** – in voller Lebensgröße.

I had just posted a letter to my cousin in Brighton – when suddenly there she was, **as large as life**, standing right in front of me! NB. *the idiom:* larger than life.

### DEATH

– **to feel/look like death/like death warmed up** – aussehen wie das leibhaftige Elend.

It was dark and freezing cold. The soldier standing guard had a splitting headache and **felt like death**.

"Let's face it – some men can **look like death warmed up** without cosmetics." (Daily Mail, 19.10.1994.)

cf. to look like a washed-out rag; to feel like a wet rag/like a bit of chewed string/like a nervous wreck; *and the opposite:* to feel/look like a million dollars; to feel like a queen/a princess; to feel as right as rain.

– **to hang/hold on like grim death** – sich verzweifelt an etwas klammern; sich mit aller Macht gegen ein Unglück stemmen.

The captain of the storm-tossed ship later told reporters that they had been **hanging on like grim death**.

– **as dark as death** – bedrohlich.

The burglar's car was parked on the shady side of the old supermarket and looked **as dark as death**.

– **as pale as death** – bleich wie der Tod, todbleich; käsebleich; kreidebleich. *Used only to describe someone's face.*

The sailor's wife turned **as pale as death** on receiving the telegram. cf. as pale as pastry.

– **as ugly as death** – häßlich wie die Nacht.

"I bring destruction" Smallpox replied. "No matter how beautiful a woman is, once she has looked at me **she becomes as ugly as death**." (The Fourth Horseman by Andrew Nikiforuk, 1992.) cf. as ugly as sin; as ugly as a box of frogs.

– **as cold as death** – kühl/kalt wie der Tod.

Here is a riddle from The Hobbit by J. R. R. Tolkien, 1937:

Alive without breath,
**As cold as death**;
Never thirsty, ever drinking,
All in mail never clinking. Answer: a fish.

## GRAVE

– **as close as the grave** – verschwiegen wie ein Grab.

"You can tell her your secret. She's **as close as the grave**." cf. as close as an oyster; as close as a Kentish oyster.

to look like a ghost

**– as silent/quiet as the grave** – Grabesstille/tote Hose.

"Our town centre is **as silent as the grave** on Sunday afternoons", the teenager complained to his cousin. cf. as quiet as a mouse.

## GHOST

**– to look like a ghost** – totenbleich/käsebleich/wie ein Gespenst/ wie eine lebende Leiche/wie der Tod aussehen.

"Do you know that old man? You **look like a ghost**!" cf. to look as white as a sheet.

**– to look as white as a ghost** – schreckensbleich/totenbleich/käsebleich/weiß wie ein Gespenst aussehen.

The two young Britons looked **as white as ghosts** after being forced to spend the day in that foreign prison.

**– like a ghost town** – wie eine Geisterstadt.

After the bomb attack all the survivors fled for their lives and now Zepa is **like a ghost town**.

## HEAVEN, NIRVANA

– **like heaven on earth** – wie der Himmel auf Erden. *The phrase is often used to draw a comparison.*

After having lived in the refugee camp for two years, it seemed **like heaven on earth** for the young man to have a flat of his very own.

– **like nirvana** – wie im siebenten Himmel, wie im Paradies.

"I want to be incredibly rich and famous. It would be **like nirvana** starring in a big Hollywood movie." (Helen Mirren, a famous British actress. Daily Mail, 23.3.1994.)

– **like manna from heaven** – wie ein warmer Regen, wie eine Fügung des Himmels.

"For me to be able to take four weeks off work is **like manna from heaven**."

## GOD

– **to eat like God in France** – essen wie Gott in Frankreich.

"Let's go to the very best restaurant in town and then we can **eat like God in France**."

– **Move, swim, ride like a god** – sich wie ein junger Gott bewegen, wie ein junger Gott schwimmen, reiten; etwas perfekt machen.

Hayley adored the tall, blond Scandinavian. He **moved like a god** in her presence.

The handsome film star **rode, swam and danced like a god** and his fans were mad about him.

– **to feel like a god** – sich fühlen, als ob man Berge versetzen könnte.

After breakfast on the terrace of my luxury hotel in Jodhpur, **I feel like a god**, especially when it is time to return to the real world of teeming streets below, where the average wage is 13p a day. (Brian Jackman, Daily Mail, 9.7.1994.)

– **to treat someone like a god** – jemanden mit aller Zuvorkommenheit behandeln.

"When a guest comes to your home, he must be **treated almost like a god**. The hostess would feel really bad if people's plates weren't full all the time." (Namita Panjabi, a high-society Asian hostess. The Sunday Times, Style and Travel, 3.7.1994.)

– **to behave like a little tin god** – sich benehmen wie ein wichtigtuerischer Despot.

"Now that Mr Lee has been promoted to Inspector, he's **behaving like a little tin god**."

## ANGEL

– **to sing like an angel** – wie ein Engel singen.

"William **sings like an angel** in the school choir, but you should see him in the school playground!"

like a guardian angel

– **to have a voice like an angel** – eine Stimme haben wie ein Engel; eine überirdisch schöne Stimme haben.

"My Irish friend, Kathleen, is a wonderful singer and **has a voice like an angel**." cf. a voice as soft as a prayer.

– **to write like an angel** – schreiben wie ein Gott; göttlich/himmlisch schreiben.

I just can't put my book down. This author **writes like an angel**.

– **like a guardian angel** – wie ein Schutzengel.

A middle-aged couple who were helped by the Princess after their car broke down said yesterday that she arrived on the scene **like a guardian angel**. (Richard Kay, Daily Mail, 4.3.1994.)

## PRAYER

– **a voice as soft as a prayer** – eine sanfte und beruhigende Stimme.

In the flesh, sipping tea in her London hotel room, Hamada is the picture of demure Japanese femininity. Her **voice is as soft as a prayer**, her manners scrupulously polite. (Tony Parsons meets the Japanese woman rock star who is aiming to conquer the world by singing in English. The European, 16.9.1993.) cf. a voice like an angel; a voice as smooth as syrup/as cold as steel/like gravel.

## MIRACLE

– **like a miracle** – wie ein Wunder; wie in einem Märchen.

"To me it was **like a miracle**. I felt alive and awake for the first time since Daniel's death. I left after two hours, knowing with every fibre of my being that there is truly life after death. It gave me hope." (Christine Yorath, telling how a medium helped her finally come to terms with her son's tragic death. Daily Mail, 28.10.1993.)

## SOUL

**– like balm to one's soul** – Balsam für die Seele.

"The thing about Roddy Llewellyn is that he is an angel, a real angel. He is the kindest person you could meet. He was devoted. And that was exactly what Princess Margaret needed then. He was **like balm to her soul**." (Anne Glenconner, Daily Mail, 7.10.1993.)

*A variation:* **to act like an unguent**.

## SIN

**– as ugly as sin** – häßlich wie die Nacht/Sünde.

"Look at that model on the catwalk! She's **as ugly as sin**." cf. as ugly as death; as ugly as a box of frogs.

## BLAZES

**– as drunk as blazes** – sturzbetrunken, sternhagelvoll.

"What a terrible noise!" Rebecca said, looking out of the window. "They're all **as drunk as blazes** down there." cf. as drunk as a lord; as drunk as a fiddler.

## DEVIL

**– to drive like the devil** – wie der Teufel/Henker fahren.

"I'm not getting into the same car as you! You **drive like the devil**!" cf. to drive like a lunatic/a madman; to drive like Jehu.

## HELL

**– like going to Hell and back** – als ob man durch die Hölle geht.

"We got badly lost and ended up in a slum. It was **like going to Hell and back**. I'm so glad we've come home at last."

to drive like the devil

**– to hurt/ache like hell** – höllisch/teuflisch schmerzen.

"I hit my finger by mistake with the hammer and it **hurt like hell**."

Poor Mrs Lightburn is ill in bed with flu and she says her muscles are **aching like hell**.

**– to work like hell** – arbeiten wie ein Wahnsinniger/Verrückter/Berserker.

The writer **worked like hell** to finish the manuscript in time for the publisher. cf. to work like a dog/a Trojan/a slave.

**– Hell hath no fury like a woman scorned** – nichts ist vergleichbar mit dem Zorn einer zurückgewiesenen Frau.

"The Maltese Angel by Catherine Cookson. **Hell hath no fury like a woman scorned** when a Durham farmer marries a music hall dancer instead of the woman who expected to be his bride. Cookson very much on form." (Book Review by Maris Ross, Daily Mail, 12.11.1993.)

**– as black as hell/as black as Hades** – schwarz wie die Hölle/der Teufel.

“I think there is a storm coming up. It is **as black as hell** out there.” cf. pitch black; as black as soot/tar/coal/ebony.

**– as sure as hell/death** – ohne jeden Zweifel; so sicher wie das Amen in der Kirche.

“**He’s sure as hell** going to kill himself if he doesn’t stop smoking.” cf. as sure as a gun; as sure as eggs is eggs.

**– to be as angry as hell** – vor Wut kochen; furchtbar wütend sein.

Mr Campbell was **as angry as hell** when he woke up to find that garden thieves had stolen his four rose bushes during the night.

**– to be as guilty as hell/sin** – absolut schuldig/verantwortlich sein.

“The police told me the boys were **as guilty as hell** but were too young to be punished.”

**– as tricky as hell** – verflucht kompliziert/komplex/schwierig.

“The gunman at the bank has taken some customers hostage and the situation is **as tricky as hell**”, the policeman told the inspector.

**– to be as frustrated as hell** – furchtbar/total enttäuscht sein.

Prince Charles remained convinced that his engagement to Diana was a “bloody awful mistake” that would only be compounded in marriage but he couldn’t convince the Queen or his father; in fact he couldn’t convince anyone at the Palace. **“He was as frustrated as hell.”** (Behind Palace Doors by Nigel Dempster and Peter Evans, 1993.)

**– as weird as hell** – höchst unheimlich; keinesfalls geheuer.

The American tourists found their stay in the haunted house **as weird as hell**.

**– as peculiar as hell** – äußerst seltsam/eigenartig.

“I just can’t understand this experiment”, the scientist groaned. “It’s **as peculiar as hell**.”

– **as lonely as hell** – total/vollkommen einsam.

The hermit has been living in this cave all by himself for two years. He must be **as lonely as hell**.

*Variations:* **as curious/shrewd/cunning** etc. **as hell**.

## DISASTER

– **like a disaster waiting to happen** – als ob man ein Unglück herausfordern würde.

That oil tanker was so old. No wonder it sprang a leak. It was **like a disaster waiting to happen**.

– **to look like a disaster in the making** – so aussehen, als bahne sich eine Katastrophe an.

One breakdown was bad enough. Two breakdowns in two days is **looking like a disaster in the making**. The new train will have to be completely overhauled.

## TROUBLE

– **to look/sound like trouble** – nach Ärger aussehen/klingen.

When the gang of skinheads entered the pub at closing time, the landlord sighed: "**This looks like trouble**. I had better telephone the police."

## SHOCK

– **to come like a sudden shock** – wie ein plötzlicher/unerwarteter Schock kommen.

After the heat of the Italian sun, the icy coldness of the grotto **came like a sudden shock**.

## 6. Trees and Flowers – *Bäume und Blumen*

### FLOWER

– **as welcome as flowers in May** – willkommen wie der Frühling/ wie die erste Maisonne.

"We paid a surprise visit to our old school teacher and she made us **as welcome as flowers in May**." cf. as welcome as water in one's shoes.

– **to smell like a flower/flowers** – nach Blumen duften.

The yacht was all ready for the party and **smelt like flowers**. cf. to smell like a perfume factory; to smell like a sewer.

### THORN

– **to be like a thorn in one's flesh** – jemandem ein Dorn im Auge/ Pfahl im Fleisch sein.

Our neighbour's loud pop music was **like a thorn in our flesh**. cf. like a stone in the shoe.

as welcome as flowers in May

## DAISY

– **as fresh as a daisy/as fresh as daisies** – frisch wie der junge Morgen; taufrisch.

After a light dinner and a good night's sleep, the ballet dancer felt **as fresh as a daisy**.

## WALLFLOWER

– **like a wallflower** – wie ein Mauerblümchen.

"My daughter, Angela, always comes with me to lots of balls. She never sits there **like a wallflower** but spends the whole evening dancing with her admirers."

## BEANSTALK

– **to grow like a beanstalk** – wachsen wie eine Bohnenstange.

"He is so tall, isn't he? He's **growing like a beanstalk**!" cf. to look like a string bean.

## GRASS

– **as perennial as the grass** – unvergänglich; unendlich dauerhaft und beständig.

Especially do not feign affection.
Neither be cynical about **love**
for in the face of all aridity
and disenchantment
**it is as perennial as the grass**.

(Desiderata was written by Indiana poet Max Ehrman in 1927.)

## GREEN BAY TREE

– **to flourish/spread like a green bay-tree** – wachsen/gedeihen/ sich ausbreiten wie Unkraut.

The idea of accompanying a lady to bed after she has consumed three pints of cider, two Drambuies and two vodkas and fallen into a rose bush has no appeal for me at all. But I suppose it is whatever turns you on. I wonder how much the new sex harassment industry, which **flourishes** on university campuses **like the green bay tree** is to blame for all this. (Keith Waterhouse, Daily Mail, 21.10.1993.)

## OAK

– **as sturdy as an oak** – stark wie ein Baum.

"It's no wonder your child is never ill. He's **as sturdy as an oak**."

## WILLOW

– **as slim as a willow** – schlank und rank wie eine Tanne.

The young student had long brown hair and was **as slim as a willow**. NB. a willowy figure.

## LEAF

– **to tremble/shake like a leaf** – wie Espenlaub zittern.

The coward was **trembling like a leaf**.

After her five minute ride on the roller-coaster, Marion came off it **shaking like a leaf**. cf. to tremble like jelly.

– **as light as a leaf** – leicht wie eine Feder, federleicht.

The young boy was floating contentedly on the water, **as light as a leaf**. cf. as light as a feather; as light as a cork.

## LOG

– **to sleep like a log/top** – wie ein Stein/Murmeltier schlafen.

"It's been a hard day's night, I should be **sleeping like a log**." (The Beatles, 1964.)

After working so hard in the garden all day, Brian **slept like a log**. cf. to sleep like a babe.

to sleep like a log

– **to be as easy as falling off a log** – praktisch von alleine funktionieren, kinderleicht sein.

"Using the new electric lawn mower is **as easy as falling off a log**." cf. as easy as shelling peas/as pie/as winking/as ABC; *and the opposite:* as easy as juggling with soot/as nailing jelly to the wall.

## PLANK

– **as thick as a plank/as two planks/as two short planks** – dumm wie Bohnenstroh.

**"I'm as thick as a plank"**, Albert moaned, after noticing all his careless arithmetic mistakes.

If anyone ever had the gift of making people feel good, it is this young mother who never passed her O-levels, and once described herself **as 'thick as two planks'**. Indeed, in her case it is more than a gift – it amounts to a kind of genius. (Paul Johnson writing about Princess Diana, Daily Mail, 4.12.1993.)

"Whyever did you give the shop assistant your secret credit card number? You're **as thick as two short planks**!"

## STICK

**– as cross as two sticks** – sehr schlecht gelaunt.

"You had better keep out of Paul's way, Susan. He's **as cross as two sticks** this morning." cf. as cross as a bear with a sore head.

**– as thin as a stick/stick-thin** – dünn wie eine Bohnenstange.

On television we were shocked to see pictures of **stick-thin** refugees. *Variations:* **matchstick-thin; whip-thin; gossamer-thin**. cf. drainpipe-thin; as thin as a rake; wafer-thin; paper-thin.

## FUNGUS

**– to spread like a fungus** – sich ausbreiten wie Fußpilz.

Linguists have spent four years among the youngsters of Milton Keynes to prove the existence of a new melting-pot accent which is **spreading like a fungus**. (Keith Waterhouse, Daily Mail, 4.8.1994.)

## WEEDS

**– to grow/spread/thrive like weeds** – sich wie Unkraut verbreiten/wachsen; sich wie Kaninchen vermehren.

"There is a crazy demand for his products. His **business will grow like weeds**."

Ireland's geography offered the potato a pleasant residence. The New World root took advantage of the cool weather and deep crumbly soil to **thrive like a weed**. (The Fourth Horseman by Andrew Nikiforuk, 1992.) cf. to breed like rabbits.

### HOPS

– **as mad as hops** – stinkwütend, stinksauer. *An American simile.*

“The gardener was **as mad as hops** when he saw the dogs chasing each other on his flower-bed.” *Variations:* as mad as a hornet/a wet hen.

### VINE

– **to cling like a vine** – sich wie eine Klette (an etwas/jemanden) hängen.

Sadly, the marriage ended in divorce because the husband could not bear the way his wife **clung to him like a vine**. cf. to cling like a limpet.

## 7. Animals – *Tiere*

### ANIMALS

– **to behave/treat like an animal** – sich wie ein wildes Tier benehmen/verhalten.

They have **behaved like animals**; not even the youngest children were spared. *A variation:* to roam the streets **like wild animals**.

“I am a prisoner-of-war and the guards are **treating us like animals**”, moaned the young soldier.

cf. treat like dogs/whipped dogs; treat like dirt/a toe-rag/a leper; treat as a pariah; *and the opposite:* to be treated like a king; treat like a celebrity; treat like gold.

### DOG

– **as tired as a dog/dog-tired** – hundemüde.

“I’m **dog-tired** after sweeping all that snow away.”

– **like a sick dog/as sick as a dog** – hundsmiserabel.

Thomas and Jimmy had far too much to drink at Emma's party and when they got back home they were both **as sick as dogs**. cf. as sick as a parrot. *A variation:* **as sick as a cat**.

– **to look like a dog's dinner/to dress up like a dog's dinner** – *etwa:* ganz schrecklich aussehen.

Wherever did you get those dreadful clothes? You **look like a dog's dinner**!" cf. to look like nothing on earth.

– **to treat like a dog/whipped dog** – jemanden wie einen Hund behandeln.

The children's home was closed down after it was discovered that the children there were **treated like whipped dogs**.
cf. treat like animals/dirt/a toe-rag/a leper; treat as a pariah.

– **to work like a dog** – arbeiten wie ein Pferd/Kuli/wie verrückt.

It's been a hard days night and I've been **working like a dog** ... (The Beatles, 1964.)

The refugees found work on the black market but they had to **work like dogs** for very little pay.

cf. to work like a horse/like beavers.

– **to die like a dog** – wie ein Hund verrecken/krepieren.

The young soldiers were no match for the experienced enemy and they **died like dogs**. cf. to die like flies.

– **like a dog in the manger** – *etwa:* anderen nichts gönnen/abgeben; mißgünstig sein.

Come on, let her borrow some of your books. You can't read all your books at once. Don't be **like a dog in the manger**."

– **as happy as a dog with two tails** – überglücklich.

"Look at little Jennifer unwrapping her Christmas presents. She's **as happy as a dog with two tails**." cf. as happy as Larry; as happy as a sandboy/a lark/a pig in horseshit.

– **as tenacious as a bulldog** – hartnäckig/beharrlich wie eine Bulldogge.

"It doesn't bother Simon that he wasn't elected as chairman. He'll try again next year. You know he's **as tenacious as a bulldog**."

## CAT

– **to fight like cat and dog** – wie Hund und Katze leben.

I'm afraid we can't have the twins in the same group at Kindergarten. They are always **fighting like cat and dog**." *A variation:* **to fight like ferrets in a sack**.

– **like a cat on hot bricks** – als ob man auf glühenden Kohlen sitzt; wie die Katze auf dem heißen Blechdach.

The nervous mother said to her child: "Can't you sit still, Susan. You're **like a cat on hot bricks**!" *Variations:* **to be as jumpy as a one-legged cat in a sandbox; like a cat on a hot tin roof**.

– **to look like the cat that swallowed the cream/has been at the cream** – *etwa:* in Hochstimmung/sehr mit sich zufrieden sein.

"I can see that you won the first prize for your flower arrangement, Sally. You **look like the cat that swallowed the cream**." *An American variation:* **to look like the cat that ate/swallowed the canary**.

– **to be like a cat with nine lives** – nicht totzukriegen sein.

"My son, Graham, has had so many accidents", Mrs Tiller moaned, "but luckily he's **like a cat with nine lives** and has always recovered very quickly."

– **to run around like a scalded cat** – in großer Hast kopflos und ohne System agieren; kopflos wie ein Huhn herumrennen.

"She's been **running around like a scalded cat** trying to get the house ready for her mother-in-law." cf. to run around like a blue-arsed fly; to run around like a headless chicken.

– **to look/be like something the cat brought in** – *etwa:* unordentlich, unappetitlich aussehen/unattraktiv erscheinen.

"Put bluntly, to most men and women, the Treaty of Maastricht is about **as appetising as something the cat brought in**." (Daily Mail, Comment, 22.7.1993.) cf. to look like a scarecrow; to look like a tramp; to look like a washed-out rag.

– **to fight like a wild cat** – wie ein Löwe kämpfen.

Police say that the shoplifter **fought like a wild cat** before collapsing. *A variation:* **to thrash about like a wild man**; cf. to fight like a tiger/tigress.

## KITTEN

– **as weak as a kitten** – schlapp wie ein ungestärkter Kragen; sehr schwach.

"After her operation, she felt **as weak as a kitten**."

– **as nervous as a kitten** – ängstlich wie ein junges Kätzchen; nervös/unruhig.

"Robert's new boss was due to arrive any minute and he was **as nervous as a kitten**." cf. as nervous as a rabbit.

– **as playful as a kitten** – verspielt wie ein Kätzchen.

"The little girl was **as playful as a kitten** after her operation. It had been a huge success." cf. as frisky as a lamb; as playful as a two-year-old. *A variation:* **as playful as a puppy**.

## HORSE

– **to sniff the air like an old war horse** – einen Krieg/Konflikt erspüren/vorausahnen.

"My grandfather has been **sniffing the air like an old war horse**. He has been watching the news on television all day."

– **to work like a horse** – arbeiten wie ein Pferd/Stier.

"It's time you had a rest; you've been **working like a horse** all the afternoon." cf. to work like a dog; to work like beavers/like a slave/like a Trojan/like hell/like magic/like a dream.

– **to eat like a horse** – einen Bärenhunger haben und entsprechend essen; fressen wie ein Scheunendrescher.

"I don't know how Melanie can be so thin", the plump girl muttered enviously, "she **eats like a horse**!" cf. to eat like a pig.

– **as strong as a horse** – bärenstark/sehr widerstandsfähig.

The doctor gave us the good news that our mother is **as strong as a horse**. cf. as strong as an ox.

She eats like a horse.

– **like locking the stable door after the horse has bolted** – *etwa:* als ob man erst handelt, nachdem das Kind in den Brunnen gefallen ist.

The boarding school should have allowed its children to have the measles vaccine. Now there is a measles epidemic, and it's too late to inject the children. Doing it now would be **like locking the stable door after the horse has bolted**.
*A morbid variation:* **like taking the temperature of a corpse**.

## MULE and DONKEY

– **as stubborn/obstinate as a mule/as obstinate as a donkey** – störrisch wie ein Esel.

"My father wants to have a swimming-pool in our garden and no one can change his mind. He's **as stubborn as a mule**."

## COW

– **as stolid as a cow** – stoisch wie eine Kuh, phlegmatisch.

"Your daughter has just gone out with a punk and you're just sitting there, reading your newspaper! You are **as stolid as a cow**."

– **as expressionless as the face of a cow** – völlig ausdrucksloses Gesicht; Pokerface.

Vincent's broad face was placid and **as expressionless as the face of a cow**. (Watchers by Dean Koontz, 1987.)

– **as nimble as a cow in a cage** – schwerfällig wie ein Elefant.

"I don't think we should dance the waltz next. You're **as nimble as a cow in a cage**." cf. as nimble as an eel in a sandbag; *and the opposite:* as nimble as ninepence.

– **as slender in the middle, as a cow in the waist** – dick wie eine Tonne; pummelig/fett.

"It might not be a good idea to buy that bikini. You're **as slender in the middle, as a cow in the waist**."

## BULL

– **like a bull in a china shop** – wie ein Elefant im Porzellanladen.

"Don't take any notice of my big brother. He's very good-hearted but he's always crashing around **like a bull in a china shop**."

– **a bull-like neck** – ein Stiernacken.

The old man sat on a dias next to a life-size stone effigy of the Buddha, and Chompa thought how alike they were: the same bulk, the same **bull-like neck** and shoulders, the same benign expression. (Little Buddha by Gordon McGill, 1994.) cf. a swan-like neck.

## OX

– **as strong as an ox** – stark wie ein Bär.

Kathleen's husband was tall and muscular and as **strong as an ox**. He managed to carry the chest of drawers up the stairs all by himself. cf. as strong as a horse.

## SHEEP

– **to be like sheep/to follow like sheep/like a flock of sheep** – wie ein Lamm sein/jemandem folgen; Kadavergehorsam haben.

"As soon as the trade union leader set off towards the police cordon, the rest of the strikers **followed like a flock of sheep**."

"Train surfing has mushroomed. It seems to have caught kids' imaginations. **Children are like sheep** and they will do what their friends say." (Alan Gadd, a schools-liaison officer who warns young people of the dangers of train surfing. Daily Mail, 14.8.1994.)

– **as silly as a sheep** – dumm wie Bohnenstroh.

"You've subtracted all these sums instead of adding them up! You are **as silly as a sheep**!" cf. as silly as a goose; NB. *the idiom:* to look sheepish.

## LAMB

**– like a lamb/as meek as a lamb** – sanft wie ein Lamm, lammfromm.

"It must have been a terrible shock to Jason when I told him he would have to give up his room, but he **took it like a lamb**."

"Hannah lets him boss her around and she never complains. She's **as meek as a lamb**."

**– as frisky as a lamb** – verspielt wie eine junge Katze/ein Kätzchen.

"What a sweet little puppy you've got. He's **as frisky as a lamb**."
*Variation:* **as playful as a puppy, as frisky as a two-year-old.**

**– as gentle/mild as a lamb** – sanft wie ein Lamm.

"You needn't be afraid of the doctor. She's **as gentle as a lamb**."
*Variation:* **as gentle as a dove.**

**– like a lamb to the slaughter/slaughter-house** – wie ein Lamm, das zur Schlachtbank geführt wird.

"Most of the time tourists to that beautiful but very poor island **are like lambs to the slaughter**; they are always being robbed and attacked."

## GOAT

**– as sure-footed as a goat** – trittsicher wie eine Bergziege.

"Just look at that mountain-climber! He's **as sure-footed as a goat**."

## PIG

**– as happy as a pig in horseshit** – glücklich und selbstzufrieden.

The computer fanatic found himself a job in a very famous computer firm and was **as happy as a pig in horseshit**.

– **to look/stare/squeal like a stuck pig** – wie ein abgestochenes Schwein schreien, vor Furcht erstarrt sein.

“Don’t just stand there **looking like a stuck pig**. Get the firemen!”

– **to eat like a pig** – essen/fressen wie ein Schwein.

“Your little brother is **eating like a pig**. Can’t you teach him some table manners?” cf. to eat like a horse.

– **as fat as a pig** – fett wie ein Schwein/eine Sau.

“If you eat all that chocolate, you’ll end up being **as fat as a pig**!” cf. to look like the back end of a tram.

– **as greedy as a pig** – gierig wie ein Schwein.

“Don’t take all these nuts. We want some too. You’re **as greedy as a pig**!”

– **to grunt like a pig** – wie ein Schwein grunzen.

The fat boy could hardly make it up the steep hill and was **grunting like a pig**.

– **to sweat like a pig/like pigs** – wie ein Affe/wie verrückt schwitzen.

The soldiers had to make their way through the jungle in the midday heat. They were soon **sweating like pigs**.

– **like a pig in a poke** – wie die Katze im Sack.

“Don’t buy that computer from the car-boot sale. You just can’t tell if it works or not. It’s **like a pig in a poke**.”

– **like pigs in clover** – wie die Maden im Speck.

“Those loud-mouthed Thompsons won the lottery jackpot last month and have been **like pigs in clover** ever since.”

– **as filthy as a pigsty** – aussehen wie in einer Räuberhöhle/in einem Schweinestall/wie bei Hempels unter dem Tisch.

"When Mary saw the students' kitchen she wrinkled up her nose and said it was **as filthy as a pigsty**."

– **to have pig-like eyes** – gierige Augen/Schweinsäuglein haben.

The antique dealer who came to look around the widow's house was small and plump, with cunning, **pig-like eyes**.

## FOX

– **as sly as a fox** – schlau wie ein Fuchs.

"You won't take him in with such a story. He's **as sly as a fox**."

– **as crafty/cunning as a fox** – listig/verschlagen wie ein Fuchs.

"Make sure you read the contract through very thoroughly. Mr Jones is **as cunning as a fox**."

*A variation:* **as cunning as a weasel**.

– **to be after someone like a fox after a goose** – hinter jemandem her sein wie der Teufel hinter der Seele. *An American simile.*

"If Sly Bill finds out what you've done, he's going to **be after you like a fox after a goose**."

– **as bad as** – ebenso/genauso schlimm wie ...

Fox-hunting in England is just **as bad as** bull-fighting in Spain. NB. *the opposite:* **as good as**.

## WOLF

– **as hungry as a wolf** – hungrig wie ein Wolf.

"Jessica came home **feeling as hungry as a wolf** after her day's outing at the seaside." cf. as hungry as a hunter.

– **to be like a wolf in sheep's clothing** – wie ein Wolf im Schafspelz.

That new drug is **like a wolf in sheep's clothing** – it can give you Alzheimer's disease when you are older.

## HYENA

– **to laugh like a hyena/a hyena-like laugh** – kreischend lachen wie eine Hyäne *(only of a woman)*.

We can always hear if Mrs Bridges is at a party or not – she **laughs like a hyena**. cf. to laugh like a jelly/a drain.

## DEER

– **as fast/swift as a deer** – flink wie ein Wiesel.

"Don't bother to race him. He's **as swift as a deer** and you'll never catch him up." cf. as fast/swift as a hare; as swift as a hawk. *The British roe deer can run up to 65 kph for short periods. A variation:* **as fleet as a gazelle**.

## FAWN

– **as gentle as a fawn** – sanft wie ein Reh.

"Alice, the child of my dreams ... **Loving as a dog** and **gentle as a fawn**: courteous, trustful, ready to accept the wildest impossibilities ..." (Rev. C. L. Dodgson in an 1887 essay on his heroine, Alice in Wonderland. The Sunday Times, The Culture, 6.11.1994.)

## BEAVER

– **to work like beavers/to be as industrious as a beaver** – arbeiten wie ein Pferd/wie die Ameisen/bienenfleißig sein.

The Red Cross volunteers **worked like beavers** to get the camp ready in time for the refugees. cf. to work like a dog/a horse/a slave/a Trojan, like hell/like magic, like a dream.

## HARE

– **to run like a hare, as swift as a hare, as fast as a hare** – schnell/flink wie ein Hase sein/rennen.

"The young joy-rider jumped out of the car and **ran like a hare** down the road and out of sight." cf. as fast/swift as a deer/a hawk; to run like the wind/like lightning. *Hares can reach a speed of 72 kph.*

## RABBIT

– **to breed/multiply/proliferate like rabbits/as fast as rabbits** – sich wie die Kaninchen vermehren.

"I just can't understand Mr and Mrs Jones. They are so terribly poor and yet **they are breeding like rabbits**."

The old lady lost her way inside the Town Hall and said crossly: "Bureaucrats seem to **proliferate like rabbits**."

– **as nervous as a rabbit** – nervös/ängstlich wie ein Hase.

"The new teacher was **as nervous as a rabbit** in front of her teenage pupils and forgot what she wanted to say." cf. as nervous as a kitten.

## SQUIRREL/HAMSTER

– **like a squirrel/hamster/squirrel-like** – wie ein Eichhörnchen.

"Diet is probably the main key to avoiding illness. In winter, people often stock up, **squirrel-like**, on sugary and starchy foods. But what the body needs is a natural, whole food diet rich in five nutrients – zinc, selenium and vitamins A, C and E." (Nutritionist Anthony Haines, The European, 17.12.1993.)

## RAT

– **to be as wet as a drowned rat/to look like a drowned rat** – wie ein begossener Pudel dastehen/aussehen.

"Thomas didn't want to take an umbrella with him and came home **looking like a drowned rat**."

– **like rats leaving/deserting a sinking ship** – wie Ratten, die das sinkende Schiff verlassen.

The politicians sensed that their leader was no longer powerful and began to distance themselves from him, **like rats deserting a sinking ship**.

– **to go down like a rat sandwich** – im Halse steckenbleiben.

The idea of old people paying domestic fuel tax is **going down like a rat sandwich**.

## LEMMING

– **like a lemming/lemming-like** – wie die Lemminge.

“The children were prepared to follow their sect leader **like lemmings** to the bitter end.” *It is just an old wives’tale that lemmings commit suicide by drowning.*

## MOUSE

– **as quiet/timid as a mouse** – zahm/unauffällig wie eine Maus/mucksmäuschenstill; eine graue Maus.

“Mr Philips was **as quiet as a mouse** at work”, said a colleague. “We had no idea he worked as a pop singer in the evenings.”

– **as merry as mice in malt** – fröhlich und munter wie ein Fisch im Wasser.

“The students were **as merry as mice in malt** at the graduation party.” cf. as merry as a cricket. *Variations:* **as merry as a grig/as the day is long**.

– **as poor as a church-mouse/as church-mice** – arm wie eine Kirchenmaus.

“They can’t afford to buy their son a computer. They’re **as poor as church-mice**.”

## HEDGEHOG

– **as prickly as a hedgehog** – stachlig wie ein Igel/leicht irritiert.

“You had better leave him alone. He’s **as prickly as a hedgehog** this morning.”

## TORTOISE

– **as slow as a tortoise** – langsam wie eine Schildkröte/Schnecke.

“Can’t you walk a little bit quicker? You’re **as slow as a tortoise**.” cf. as slow as a snail

## FROG

– **as ugly as a box of frogs** – häßlich wie die Nacht.

Darren wasn't too pleased when he saw that his future mother-in-law was **as ugly as a box of frogs**. cf. as ugly as sin.

## TOAD

– **as fidgety as a toad on a griddle** – wie auf heißen Kohlen; zappelig.

The little child in the doctor's waiting-room was **as fidgety as a toad on a griddle**. cf. like a hen on a hot griddle, as hot as a griddle; like a cat on hot bricks.

## PADDOCK

– **as cold as a paddock** – kalt wie ein Fisch/eiskalt.

*A* paddock *is ‚eine Kröte' or ‚ein Frosch'; and we have the corresponding phrases* **cold as a toad**, *and* **cold as a frog**.

"Here a little child I stand
Heaving up my either hand;
**Cold as paddocks** though they be,
Here I lift them up to Thee,
For a Benizon to fall
On our meat and on us all."

(Robert Herrick: A Child's Grace. *Benizon is a blessing.*)

## CHAMELEON

– **like a chameleon/chameleon-like** – wie ein Chamäleon.

The book "The Prince of Wales" by Jonathan Dimbley, lays bare details of Charles' courtship and marriage to Diana, ruthlessly reinforcing the impression of her as an unstable and **chameleon-like character**. (Richard Kay and Edward Verity, Daily Mail, 17.10.1994.)

## BAT

– **as blind as a bat** – blind wie eine Fledermaus.

"I was very insecure because I was overweight, had a twitch and was **as blind as a bat**. Then I dropped a stone, my spots disappeared, I discovered contact lenses and I got into RADA." (Louise Jameson, an actress, Daily Mail, 19.2.1994.)

– **to run like a bat out of hell** – mit einem Affenzahn/blitzschnell laufen.

The tourist got such a fright when she heard the strange noises that she ran out of the castle **like a bat out of hell**.
cf. like lightning; as quick as a flash. *A variation:* **like the clappers**.

## SNAKE

– **to hiss like a snake** – zischen wie eine Schlange.

Suddenly the attic door burst open and a large, dark shape came slowly towards me, **hissing like a snake**.

– **a snake-like voice/a voice as soft as a snake** – eine einschmeichelnde Stimme.

The sect leader told his followers in a soft, **snake-like voice** to leave their families and to have nothing more to do with them.

I heard her, too. Her voice whispered again, intimate, unpleasant, **soft as a snake**. (Mrs de Winter by Susan Hill, 1993.)

– **as quick as a snake** – schlangengleich; wendig/gelenkig wie eine Schlange.

I was sure I had caught the thief, but **quick as a snake** he wriggled out of my grasp and ran away.
cf. as quick as a flash; like lightning; as quick as thought.

– **as mean as a snake** – gemein/widerwärtig wie eine Schlange.

The leader of the gang was **as mean as a snake** and everyone was afraid of him. *A humorous variation of the above simile:* **as mean**

**as a snake with fang decay**. (Used by Dean Koontz in Lightning, 1988.)

– **a path, queue, stream,** etc. **meanders/winds like a snake** – ein Weg/Fluß etc. windet sich wie eine Schlange.

The river **meandered like a snake** through the jungle but we had to follow it or we would have got completely lost.

## ELEPHANT

– **as heavy as an elephant** – schwer wie ein Elefant.

"Don't let her sit on our new couch. She's **as heavy as an elephant**." cf. as heavy as lead.

– **as clumsy as an elephant** – ungeschickt wie ein Elefant im Porzellanladen.

"Oh, no! You've knocked the vase of flowers over. You really are **as clumsy as an elephant**." cf. like a bull in a china shop.

– **to have a memory like an elephant** – ein Gedächtnis haben wie ein Elefant; sich etwas für immer merken.

"I'll never forget how nasty you were to me at school twenty years ago. I **have a memory like an elephant**." cf. *the opposite:* a memory like a sieve.

## RHINOCEROS

– **to have a skin/a hide like a rhinoceros** – ein dickes Fell haben.

"Don't be afraid to tell him what you think. He has a **skin like a rhinoceros**." cf. skin like a peach; skin as soft as silk; skin as white as snow; skin like porcelain; NB. *the idioms:* gossamer skin; to be thick-skinned; to be thin-skinned.

## MONKEY

– **as agile as a monkey** – flink wie ein Wiesel.

"It's a pleasure to watch Mervyn on the ropes. He's **as agile as a monkey**."

**– to climb like a monkey** – klettern wie ein Affe.

The boy climbed up the tree **like a monkey**. cf. to climb like a steeplejack.

**– as cheeky as a monkey** – frech wie ein Affe; ungezogen.

The teacher punished the boy for being **as cheeky as a monkey** in class.

**– as melancholy as a sick monkey** – melancholisch, trübsinnig.

"You really mustn't stay at home all day feeling **as melancholy as a sick monkey**. Let's go for a walk." *A variation:* **as melancholy as a cat**.

**– as clever as a cartload of monkeys** – gerissen wie eine Schlange.

"It will be very difficult to catch that drug dealer. He's **as clever as a cartload of monkeys**."

## LION

**– as brave as a lion** – mutig wie ein Löwe.

"Good girl, Christine. Your operation's over and you were **as brave as a lion**."

**– as fierce as a lion** – grimmig/ungestüm/heftig wie ein Löwe.

"We really mustn't annoy our neighbour in any way. He's **as fierce as a lion**."

**– to roar like a lion** – brüllen wie ein Löwe.

"When old Mr Eliot gets really angry, you can hear him **roaring like a lion**."

**– to feel like a lion** – *etwa:* sich topfit fühlen, fit wie ein Turnschuh.

Luciano Pavarotti, the Italian tenor, who threatened to quit because of health problems, now **feels like a lion**. (Daily Mail, 16.6.1993.) cf. to feel as right as rain.

– **lion-like hair** – Löwenmähne.

Rebecca's **lion-like** hair attracted much attention and she was even able to get a job advertising shampoo. cf. hair as black as ebony; hair like silk; hair as flat as a pancake.

## TIGER

– **to fight like a tiger/tigress** – kämpfen wie eine Tigerin/ein Tiger/ein Löwe.

He **fought like a tiger** for the custody of their children.

The memoirs of the famous politician reveal that she **fought like a tigress** to get her own way.

cf. fight like a wild cat; fight like a man.

## BEAR

– **to be like a bear with a sore head/as cross as a bear with a sore head/as savage as a bear with a sore head** – in einer besonders gereizten, schlechten Stimmung sein.

"Dad is **like a bear with a sore head** this morning. I wonder what has upset him." cf. as cross a two sticks.

# 8. Birds – *Vögel*

## BIRD

– **as free as a bird** – frei wie ein Vogel/vogelfrei.

"Why is that man still **as free as a bird**? We all know that he's a burglar." cf. as free as the air; as free as the wind.

– **to go like a bird** – laufen wie geschmiert.

"I love my new car. It **goes like a bird**." cf. to go like a dream.

– **bird-like** – wie ein Vogel.

"At 40, Jung Chang has lustrous, long black hair and delicate features. There is an almost **bird-like** fragility about her which makes you ask how it was possible for this woman to survive as a Red Guard, a peasant, a "barefoot (i.e. untrained) doctor", a steel worker and an electrician before she came to Britain on one of the first scholarships from post-Maoist China." (Daily Mail, Sue Fox, 1.10.1993.)

– **to eat like a bird/sparrow/to pick at one's food like a bird** – essen wie ein Spatz.

"You won't get well if you **pick at your food like a bird**", the nurse scolded her patient.

## DUCK

– **like a sitting duck** – wie eine Zielscheibe/ein leichtes Ziel.

"That plane over there is **like a sitting duck** in the sky", the enemy pilot sniggered.

"To the muggers of Miami they are **like sitting ducks** – tourists in hire cars with bags full of holiday money. Time after time British holidaymakers have had their trip ruined almost before it has begun". (Daily Mail, 13.4.1992.)

– **like a dying duck in a thunderstorm** – wie ein begossener Pudel, wie ein sterbender Schwan.

"You do sound sorry for yourself – **like a dying duck in a thunderstorm**.

– **like water off a duck's back** – als ob man gegen eine Wand redet.

"I told Marion to be more polite to our neighbour but my words were **like water off a duck's back**." cf. like talking to a brick wall; like whistling in the wind; like spitting into the wind.

– **to take to something like a duck to water** – mühelos mit neuen Situationen fertig werden; ein Naturtalent sein.

The City stockbroker decided to give up his job and start an ostrich farm in the north of England. His friends thought he was mad but **he took to it like a duck to water**.

## CHICKEN

– **as tender as a chicken** – schwach auf der Brust.

"That office worker is **as tender as a chicken**. He won't be able to help you carry those desks and chairs."

– **like a spring chicken** – wie junges Gemüse, frisch und knackig; jemand, der für sein Alter jung aussieht.

"I don't know what you're worried about", the doctor said. "He's **like a spring chicken**." cf. like mutton dressed as lamb.

– **to run around like a headless chicken** – kopflos wie ein aufgescheuchtes Huhn herumlaufen.

"We've got ten guests coming to dinner tonight, and our poor mother is **running around like a headless chicken**!"

– **to run something like a headless chicken** – etwas konfus und unsystematisch tun/betreiben.

The manager of the Apple Tree Activity Centre **ran it like a headless chicken** and made it lose all its customers.

– **a headless chicken look** – ein perplexer, ungläubiger Gesichtsausdruck.

"You've got that **headless chicken look**," the UFO expert laughed. "Most people look like that after they've seen a flying saucer."

## HEN

– **to cluck like a hen** – mit seiner Zunge ein mißbilligendes Geräusch machen.

The teacher **clucked like a hen** and looked disapprovingly at her class.

– **like hen's teeth** – wie ein Lottogewinn.

"Promotions like this are **like hen's teeth**. Go for it, Steven!"
cf. like dragon's teeth.

– **like a hen on a hot griddle** – wie auf heißen Kohlen; ruhelos.

"Christine's boyfriend was late-coming, and she was **like a hen on a hot griddle**." cf. as fidgety as a toad on a griddle, like a cat on hot bricks.

– **like a hen with one chicken** – besorgt wie eine Glucke.

"It's not so cold outside, don't dress Jane too warmly. You're **like a hen with one chicken**."

## GOOSE

– **like grease through a goose** – *etwa:* sehr gründlich, keinen Stein auf dem anderen lassen. *An American simile.*

"We must find the missing necklace. We'll go through that house **like grease through a goose**."

## TURKEY

– **to be trussed up like a turkey** – wie ein Paket verschnüren.

"The burglars have **trussed me up like a turkey**. If only the police would come."

**– like turkeys voting for Christmas** – sich ins eigene Fleisch schneiden; selbstzerstörerisch sein/handeln.

I can't see anyone volunteering to patrol that ghetto at night. It would be **like turkeys voting for Christmas**.

## PARTRIDGE

**– as plump as a partridge** – sehr pummelig.

"I'm afraid that dress will never fit Nicola. She is as **plump as a partridge**."

## COOT

**– as stupid as a coot** – dumm wie Bohnenstroh.

"Oh no! Now we've got to pay and you've left your purse at home. You are **as stupid as a coot**!"

**– as crazy as a coot** – ein verrücktes Huhn.

"My aunt is the life and soul of any party and she's **as crazy as a coot**." *The coot's cry is a noisy mad-like cackle.*

**– as bald as a coot** – vollkommen glatzköpfig.

The little girl's grandfather was fat and jolly and **as bald as a coot**. *Variations:* **as bald as a bandicoot/as a billiard ball**.

## CROW

**– to look like a scarecrow** – wie eine Vogelscheuche/Schreckschraube aussehen.

"I can't possibly wear this dress at the ball. I shall **look like a scarecrow** in it." cf. to look like a tramp/like nothing on earth/a dog's dinner; to look like one has been dragged through a hedge backwards.

## RAVEN

– **as black as a raven/raven-black** – kohlrabenschwarz, schwarz wie ein Rabe/die Nacht.

The Flamenco dancer had **raven-black** hair and wore a striking red silk dress. cf. as black as ebony/coal/pitch/soot/tar/Hades/hell.

## DOVE

– **as gentle as a dove** – sanft und friedlich wie eine Taube.

"Patricia will make a very good nurse. She is **as gentle as a dove**." cf. as gentle as a lamb.

– **as harmless as a dove** – harmlos wie eine Taube, absolut harmlos.

"I know she's a bit strange in the head but you needn't worry. She's as **harmless as a dove**."

– **as safe as a dove-cote** – sicher wie in Abrahams Schoß.

"You can hide from the journalists in my cottage in the wood. It is **as safe as a dove-cote**."

## LARK

– **to be as happy as a lark** – quietschfidel/glücklich, sorglos und unbeschwert.

"Matthew is **as happy as a lark**, playing with his new model railway." cf. as happy as a sandboy/as a pig in horseshit/as the day is long/as happy as Larry/as happy as a dog with two tails.

## MAGPIE

– **to chatter like a magpie** – schnattern wie die Gänse/wie die Waschweiber.

"Whenever Jennifer has her friends here for the afternoon I can hear her **chattering like a magpie**."

## ALBATROSS

– to have something **hang round one's neck like an albatross** – einen Klotz am Bein haben.

Anthony Burgess's futuristic fantasy *A Clockwork Orange*, published in 1962, brought him notoriety, but it **hung round his neck like an albatross**. "It's not my favourite book, and I really wish they would think of me in relation to something else," he once said. (Daily Mail, 26.11.1993.)

"I knew the calorific content of every single food item you could think of, and it was **like an albatross around my neck**. So I decided to give it all up, eat sensibly and take lots of exercise." (Grace Hill, health and beauty editor. Fibrenetics by Gilly Smith, 1993.) cf. to hang like a millstone round one's neck.

to hang round one's neck like an albatross

## CANARY

– **to sing like a canary** – singen/auspacken/verraten.

Secret documents proved that one of the criminals **sang like a canary** to police officers.

## PARROT

– **like a parrot** – wie ein Papagei.

The schoolboy had learnt to say his Latin grammar **like a parrot** but he didn't understand any of it.

– **to be as sick as a parrot** – die Nase/Schnauze voll haben; die Faxen dicke haben. *A cliché often used by football managers and footballers.*

It was a national disaster and football fans everywhere **felt as sick as parrots**. (Bill Mouland, Daily Mail, 19.2.1994.) *Sick parrots suffering from psittacosis (parrot fever) are melancholy and dejected.*

## OWL

– **as wise as an owl** – weise/klug wie eine Eule.

"Quickly go to Martin and let him help you with your homework! You know he's **as wise as an owl**!" cf. as wise as Solomon.

– **as solemn as an owl** – *(derogatory)* ernsthaft und humorlos.

"Don't bother to play any jokes on Judy. She's **as solemn as an owl**."

## SWAN

– **as graceful as a swan** – graziös wie ein Schwan.

"I am so glad that Yvette had ballet lessons. She is **as graceful as a swan**."

– **a swan-like neck** – ein Schwanenhals.

The ice-skater stretched out her **swan-like neck** and leapt through the air. cf. bull-like neck.

## DODO

– **as dead as the dodo** – ausgerottet/ausgestorben/mausetot/absolut überholt.

"I thought that pop songs from the 1960s were as dead as the dodo, but now they seem to have made a comeback." cf. as dead as a door-nail/as a nail in a coffin/as a tent-peg/as a mouse/as a herring/ shotten herring; stone-dead. *The large bird, the dodo, became extinct on Mauritius in the 1680s.*

## PEACOCK

– **as proud/vain as a peacock** – eitel und stolz wie ein Pfau.

"Thomas was **as proud as a peacock** after being able to converse fluently in Japanese with the tourist."

## PHOENIX

– **to rise like a phoenix from the ashes** – wie ein Phönix aus der Asche aufsteigen.

"On December 21, 1989 Pan Am Flight 103 exploded over the rooftops – and Sherwood Crescent, Lockerbie, became known throughout the world. Today, the crescent itself **has risen like a phoenix from the ashes**. The rubble and wreckage have long since been cleared away and new bungalows built to replace those destroyed." (James Grylls, Daily Mail, 30.6.1993.)

## HAWK

– **as swift as a hawk** – wie ein Habicht.

"The antique dealer pounced on the valuable vase **as swift as a hawk**." cf. as swift as a deer; as swift as a hare.

– **to watch/watch over someone like a hawk** – jemanden mit Adleraugen beobachten/wie ein Schießhund/Luchs auf jemanden aufpassen.

"You must **watch that young man like a hawk**. Everyone knows that he is a thief."

After several kidnap threats, the wealthy bride was **watched over like a hawk** at her wedding ceremony.

## VULTURE

– **like a vulture** – wie die Geier.

"Those two muggers were **like vultures**," their victim moaned. "They knocked me down and stole all my money."

Mr Palmer's brothers and their wives had never bothered to visit him in the past, but now that he was dying they crowded around his bed **like vultures**.

## OSTRICH

– **to be like an ostrich with its head in the sand** – den Kopf in den Sand stecken, Vogel-Strauß-Politik betreiben.

"You must admit that you can't afford to live in such a luxurious apartment. You are like an **ostrich with its head in the sand**."

– **to have a digestion like an ostrich** – einen Magen wie eine Kuh haben, über eine absolut unerschütterliche Verdauung verfügen.

"However can he eat such strange food? He must have a **digestion like an ostrich**." *The ostrich eats indigestible things such as stones and hard objects to assist the function of its gizzard.*

## FEATHER

– **as light as a feather** – leicht wie eine Feder, federleicht.

"Lucky you, Monica. Your satchel is **as light as a feather** today!" cf. as light as a leaf; as light as a cork.

- **float like a feather** – schweben/gleiten wie eine Feder/ein Blatt im Wind.

The new plane was **floating like a feather** in the clear blue sky.

- **one's heart is floating like a feather** – sich leicht, unbeschwert und glücklich fühlen.

When Max tells her he has murdered Rebecca, how perfect was the reply: "**My heart is like a feather floating in the air.** He has never loved Rebecca." (Rebecca by Daphne du Maurier, 1938.)

### CAGE

- **like a bird in a cage** – wie ein Vogel im Käfig.

"It has become easier. In the early days it was terrible. Lee was dead, but I was left here to be blamed. **I was like a bird in a cage.**" (Marina Oswald, widow of Lee Harvey Oswald. Daily Mail, 28.11.1992.)

## 9. Fish – *Fische*

### FISH

- **to be like a fish out of water** – wie ein Fisch auf dem Trockenen sitzen/wie ein Fisch ohne Wasser. *The opposite of "munter wie ein Fisch im Wasser".*

"I'm afraid your cousin will be **like a fish out of water** in Alaska. He's used to a hot climate and he can't speak any English."

- **to swim like a fish** – schwimmen wie ein Fisch.

After only ten swimming lessons Vivien could **swim like a fish**.

to need s.th. like a fish needs a bicycle

– **to drink like a fish** – trinken/saufen wie ein Loch.

"I **drink like a fish**, neat vodka, no ice. I can get through half a bottle without feeling it and I never have hangovers." (Thelma Holt, Daily Mail, 25.8.1993.)

– **to need something like a fish needs a bicycle** –so überflüssig wie nur sonst irgend etwas sein.

The Minister of Erfurt, Thuringia's capital said: "We need the Communist party **like a fish needs a bicycle.**" (The Sunday Times, 14.1.1990.) cf. like the moth needs the candle flame.

## GOLDFISH

– **like being in a goldfish bowl** – als ob man auf einem Präsentierteller sitzt.

Being in the Centre Court royal box is **like being in a goldfish bowl**. (The Sun, 4.7.1992.)

## CLAM

- **to shut up/close up like a clam/to be as tight-mouthed as a clam** – schweigen wie ein Grab; verschwiegen sein wie ein Grab; kein Wort mehr aus jemandem herausbekommen

"Before I **close up like a clam** I'll tell you one last thing about my ex-husband."

"The prisoner won't tell us anything. He is as **tight-mouthed as a clam**".

## LIMPET

- **to cling/stick like a limpet** – wie eine Klette an jemandem hängen.

The little child **clung** to her plump and cuddly grandmother **like a limpet** and refused to let her go.

Margaret Thatcher had a few simple ideas and she **stuck** to them **like a limpet**. (Daily Mail, 23.11.1990.)

The picturesque little village **clung like a limpet** to the cliff edge of the Mediterranean island. cf. to stick/cling like a leech/a vine.

## CAVIAR

- **like caviar to the general** – als ob man Perlen vor die Säue wirft.

"The poet considered many of his poems to be like **caviar to the general**." *The word "general" in the phrase refers to the general public, not to the military rank.*

## OYSTER

- **as close as an oyster/a Kentish oyster** – verschlossen wie ein Grab.

"You can trust me with your secret. I'll be **as close as an oyster**." cf. as close as the grave.

## SARDINES

– **to be packed like sardines** – zusammengepfercht sein wie die Heringe.

"We were **packed like sardines** on the train. I could hardly move my arms."

"December 12. The boat is riddled with cockroaches and there is only one toilet which stinks. I didn't get much sleep. We **lay like sardines** on the deck on our cardboard mats." (Daily Mail, 28.6.1993.)

## EEL

– **as slippery as an eel** – glatt wie ein Aal, aalglatt/gerissen/geschmeidig.

"I couldn't get anything in writing out of him; he is **as slippery as an eel**."

– **as nimble as an eel in a sandbag** – *etwa:* steif und unbeweglich.

"I really don't know why they chose her to dance that part. She's **as nimble as an eel in a sandbag**." cf. as nimble as a cow in a cage; *and the opposite:* as nimble as ninepence.

# 10. Insects – *Insekten*

## FLY

– **to die/be dying off/drop/be killed/shot down like flies** – wie die Fliegen sterben.

Cholera is sweeping through the town and people are **dying like flies.**

It would be too risky to run away from the enemy now. They could all **be shot down like flies**.

– **to trap/catch something like a fly in amber** – etwas einfangen, festhalten.

Not a great movie, possibly not even a good one, but WHAT'S NEW PUSSYCAT? **traps** one element of the Sixties **like a fly in amber** – and always makes me chuckle. (John Marriott, Daily Mail, 20.2.1993.)

– **to run around like a blue-arsed fly** – herumlaufen wie ein aufgescheuchtes/kopfloses Huhn.

"The cellar is flooded and our father is **running around like a blue-arsed fly**, but it's hopeless. Everything is dripping wet." cf. to run around like a scalded cat/like a headless chicken.

– **to fall like flies** – schwach werden.

The lead singer in the West End musical is so handsome and has such a beautiful voice. The girls just **fall like flies** when they see him.

– **to descend/be like flies on or around someone** – sich wie ein Schwarm Fliegen auf jemanden stürzen.

If Caroline had known he was leaving the jurisdiction of the English court, the lawyers would have been on him **like flies**. (Hotel Pastis by Peter Mayle, 1993.)

## BUTTERFLY

– **butterfly-like** – flatterhaft/unstet wie ein Schmetterling.

The efforts of the philosopher, Bernard-Henry Levy, to be taken seriously have in the past floundered owing to the **butterfly-like** range of his interests. (Tony Allen-Mills, The Sunday Times, 29.5.1994.)

## MOTH

– **like a moth that flies round a light/like moths around a light** – wie Motten, die das Licht umschwärmen.

The children gathered eagerly around the box of chocolates **like moths around a light**.

– **to need something like the moth needs the candle flame** – überflüssig sein wie ein Kropf.

Prince Charles's safety now lies in silence, not self-promotion. His opinions **need publicity like the moth needs the candle flame**. (Daily Mail Comment, 30.6.1994.) cf. like a fish needs a bicycle.

## BEE

– **as busy as a bee/to work like bees** – bienenfleißig.

Yvonne was **as busy as a bee** all day and managed to finish the decorating before it got dark.

The road-sweepers can **work like bees** if they get paid enough. *Variations:* **as busy as an ant; as busy as a bandicoot; as busy as a one-armed paperhanger with the itch** *(an American simile)*.

– **to be as flexible as a bee in a honey pot** – völlig unflexibel sein.

"Whyever can't you change those appointments around?" Angela groaned. "You are **as flexible as a bee in a honey pot**!"

– **to draw someone like bees to a honey pot** – von etwas angezogen werden wie die Motten vom Licht/wie von einem Magneten/etwas umschwärmen wie die Motten das Licht.

Thanks to all the publicity, journalists have been **swarming round the politician like bees round a honey pot**.

One could tell at once that she was a bit of a tart and all the boys were **after her like bees round a honey pot.** cf. to draw like a magnet; to draw like iron filings to a magnet.

## BUG

– **as snug as a bug (in a rug)** – wohlig, gemütlich und bequem.

"You look **as snug as a bug** sitting there in your favourite armchair in front of the fire and sipping your hot cocoa."

## FLEA

– **as fit as a flea** – gesund und munter wie ein Fisch im Wasser/ kerngesund.

"Jason was **as fit as a flea** after his walking holiday in the Lake District." cf. as fit as a fiddle.

– **to be all over someone like fleas on a dog** – sich wie die Aasgeier auf jemanden stürzen.

The reporters found out who the winner of the 17 million pound lottery jackpot was and were soon **all over him like fleas on a dog.** cf. to be all over someone like a bad rash.

## SNAIL

– **as slow as a snail** – langsam wie eine Schnecke.

"You really must hurry up. The doctor is waiting for you. You're **as slow as a snail**." cf. as slow as a tortoise.

## LEECH

– **to stick/cling like a leech** – wie eine Klette (an jemandem) hängen.

"Whenever we invite our former neighbour to stay with us, we can never get rid of him. He **sticks like a leech**." *A leech is a blood-*

*sucking worm. Leeches are still being used by some doctors in Britain to this very day. The action of blood sucking has beneficial effects on damaged skin.* cf. to cling/stick like a limpet.

## CRICKET

– **as merry/chirpy as a cricket** – glücklich, fröhlich und ausgelassen.

"Mr Higgens had just won £100 playing Bingo and he was **as merry as a cricket**." cf. as merry as a grig/as mice in malt.

– **as lively as a cricket** – quicklebendig.

"It's amazing how well my grandfather plays with my little son. He's **as lively as a cricket**."

## LOCUST

– **to swarm like locusts around someone** – wie Motten das Licht umschwärmen/wie die Heuschrecken über jemanden herfallen.

When they heard that wealthy Mr Travers was writing his will, his poor relations **swarmed like locusts around him.** cf. like vultures.

## TARANTULA

– **eyelashes like tarantulas/spiders' legs** – Augenwimpern wie Spinnenbeine.

"The young model had long blonde hair, **eyelashes like tarantulas** and bright red lipstick smeared thickly on her lips."

## STICK INSECT

– **to look like a stick insect** – wie eine Bohnenstange aussehen.

The clothes designers only design clothes for very thin models. Do they expect us all to **look like stick insects?**

Working for Hammond Hughes (a model agency which specialises in larger women) definitely puts less pressure on a girl to look like

to look like a stick insect

**a stick insect,** and all the models are less paranoid." (Heather Mills, a model talking to Tracey Harrison, Daily Mail, 26. 7. 1994.) cf. as thin as a rake; drainpipe-thin; stick-thin.

## 11. The Body – *Der Körper*

### BONE

– **as dry as a bone/bone dry** – knochentrocken/staubtrocken.

"I can't grow anything in my garden. The soil is **bone dry**."

"I just can't understand why you want to trek through the desert at this time of year. It's boiling hot and **as dry as a bone**."

*The same simile can be used humorously for wanting a drink very badly:* "Let's stop at the pub; I'm **as dry as a bone**." cf. as dry as dust.

– **bone idle** – ein fauler Hund/Knochen.

I wish I had never employed that gardener. He's **bone idle**. NB. *the idiom:* lazy bones.

## SKELETON

– **like a skeleton at a feast** – wie das leibhaftige schlechte Gewissen.

The refugee was the guest of honour at the charity banquet and was **like a skeleton at a feast**.

## SKIN

– **like a second skin** – wie eine zweite Haut.

"Maggie's so funny," Anna joked. "She jumped into the bath with her jeans on so that they would **cling to her like a second skin**!" cf. to fit like a glove.

## BLOOD

– **like getting/drawing blood from a stone** – als ob man einen Stein zum Weinen bringt; als ob man einem nackten Mann in die Tasche greift.

Eliciting a description of her beauty routine will probably be easier in a few years' time, when she's talked to hundreds of journalists and has it all off pat. In the meantime, **it's like drawing blood from a stone**. (Adriane Pielou on model Niki Taylor, YOU magazine, 25.10.1992.) NB. *the idiom:* you can't get blood out of a stone.

## GALL

– **as bitter as gall** – bitter wie Galle.

"Rachel failed her History exam last year and she's been **as bitter as gall** ever since." NB. *the idiom:* gall and wormwood.

## HEAD

– **to want/need something like a hole in the head** – überflüssig sein wie ein Kropf.

"You **need** another computer game **like you need a hole in the head**, Alex. You should spend more time reading your school-books."

## FACE

– **like a slap in the face** – wie ein Schlag ins Gesicht.

"Margaret Thatcher's gone." The stark statement **stung me like a slap in the face**. (The Bastards by Teresa Gorman, MP for Billericay 1993.)

To the National Front's leader Jean-Marie Le Pen, every note of jazz is **like a slap in the face**. (Roman Rollnick, The European, 20. 2. 1992.) *A variation: on the telephone:* **like a slap in the ear.**

## EYES

– **as easy as winking** – wie im Schlaf, kinderleicht.

"I can knit with my eyes closed. It's **as easy as winking**." cf. as easy as falling off a log/as pie/as ABC/as shelling peas.

## NOSE

– **as plain as the nose on someone's face** – das sieht doch ein Blinder mit dem Krückstock; klar wie Kloßbrühe.

"Did the window-cleaner steal the radio? Of course he did! It's as **plain as the nose on your face**." cf. as plain as a pikestaff.

## TEETH

– **like drawing teeth** – zum Mäusemelken.

Our boss, Mrs Richardson, is so sure of herself that when she makes a mistake **it's like drawing teeth** to get an apology from her.

## NECK

– **to hang like a millstone round one's neck** – jemandem ein Klotz am Bein sein. *A variation:* **like a burden round one's neck**.

The scale of the overmanning at Mercedes is reminiscent of British Leyland in its worst days: great snowdrifts of white-collar staff, whole regiments of blue-collar workers who are now surplus to requirements and **hang like millstones round the** company's **neck**. (Graham Turner, Daily Mail, 5.3.1993.)

"Martin saved our firm from bankruptcy three times and he won't let us forget it. Always being reminded of it is **like a burden round our necks**." cf. hang round someone's neck like an albatross.

## BACK

– **like the backside of nowhere** – wie am Ende/Arsch der Welt.

Having lived in London all her life, Tracy was horrified when her husband inherited a cottage in a tiny village. It seemed **like the backside of nowhere**.

– **to look like the back end of a tram/bus** – häßlich sein wie die Nacht/aussehen wie eine Vogelscheuche.

"I don't think we should employ that waitress to work in our restaurant. She **looks like the back end of a tram**!" cf. to look like a bag lady/like a dog's dinner/like a scarecrow/like a tramp.

## ARM

– **to need something like a shot in the arm** – etwas als Stimulans brauchen.

After working all day in the office, the boss needed a smile from his favourite secretary **like a shot in the arm**.

## HAND

– **to know something like the back of one's hand** – etwas in- und auswendig wissen/kennen.

The tourist guide proudly told her listeners that she **knew London like the back of her hand.**

## SHADOW

– **to follow someone around like a shadow** – jemandem wie ein Schatten folgen.

Sophie hero-worshipped her elder brother and **followed him around like a shadow**.

to follow s.o. around like a shadow

## 12. Illnesses and Ailments – *Krankheiten und Leiden*

### VIRUS

– **to spread like a virus** – sich wie ein Virus/in Windeseile verbreiten.

The Milton Keynes Kids' lingo is expected to **spread like a virus.** (John Osborne, The Mail on Sunday, 7.8.1994.)

### CONTAGION/DISEASE

– **to spread like a contagion/disease** – sich wie ein Lauffeuer verbreiten.

Although the headmaster tried to keep it a secret, news that the Biology teacher had stolen some valuable library books **spread like a contagion** around the school.

"This pursuit of greyness, this preference for the undistinguished and indistinguishable, is **spreading like a disease** through our society." (Paul Johnson, a leading historian, Daily Mail, 30.4.1994.)

cf. to spread like wildfire; to spread like a bush-fire; to spread like a rash; to spread like a fungus.

### PLAGUE

– **to avoid something like the plague** – meiden wie die Pest.

I **avoid** all insects **like the plague** but I love looking at them in the zoo where they are safely behind glass.

If you want to write well, you must **avoid** clichés and jargon **like the plague**.

### RASH

– **to be over somebody like a rash/like a bad rash/to spread like a rash** – jemanden nicht mehr losbekommen/am Hals haben.

Diana felt “fairly intimidated” by the atmosphere on board the royal yacht Britannia during Cowes Week. She found Charles’ friends too friendly and too knowing. “**They were all over me like a bad rash**”, she told her friends. (Diana: Her True Story by Andrew Morton, 1992.) cf. to be all over someone like fleas on a dog; to spread like wildfire/a bush-fire/a fungus/a virus/a contagion/a disease.

## LEPER

– **to feel like/treat someone like a leper** – sich wie ein Aussätziger fühlen/jemanden wie einen Aussätzigen behandeln.

Skin Deep is a nation-wide network for sufferers of unsightly skin conditions, disfiguring burns and scars. “In the company of other sufferers, you no longer **feel like a leper**. The sense of liberation is tremendous.” (Ashley Medicks, the founder of Skin Deep, Daily Mail, 27.12.1994.)

## CANCER

– **to invade like cancer** – sich ausbreiten wie ein Krebsgeschwür.

Political correctness is beginning to **invade English like a cancer**. Our language is not an artificial construct. It is a living thing. We should cherish it as we would our own flesh and blood. (Daily Mail commenting on the Open University which has ordained that the phrase ‘non-self body’ be used instead of ‘foreign body’. 6.12.1993.)

## SORE

– **to stick out like a sore thumb** – total aus dem Rahmen fallen; durch irgend etwas besonders auffallen, anders sein.

“Why are you wearing a mini-dress when the rest of us are wearing long evening dresses? You **stick out like a sore thumb**!”

## CARBUNCLE

– **like a monstrous carbuncle** – wie ein monströses Geschwür.

"... but what is proposed is **like a monstrous carbuncle** on the face of a much loved and elegant friend." (Prince Charles invented this simile when he criticised the proposed design for the new wing of the National Gallery in London at the 150th anniversary dinner of the Royal Institute of British Architects on 30th May, 1984.)

## DEAF

– **to be as deaf as a door-post** – stocktaub sein.

*Sometimes said of a person who is not conscious of his deafness.* "She's **as deaf as a door-post** but she doesn't want to wear her new hearing aid." *A variation:* **as deaf as an adder**.

## WOUND

– **like a wound/to fester like an open/internal wound** – wie eine offene Wunde (schwären), anfällig wie eine offene Wunde sein.

New germs such as HIV continue to kill unequal numbers of aboriginal people because the smallpox legacy of poor health still **festers like an open wound**. (The Fourth Horseman by Andrew Nikiforuk, 1992.)

What he would say he cannot say to this woman whose **openness is like a wound**, whose youth is not mortal yet. (The English Patient by Michael Ondaatje, 1992.)

## MEDICINE

– **to go through something like a dose of salts** – etwas sehr schnell und wirksam tun.

"The mathematician went through his income tax documents **like a dose of salts**." *From Epson Salts which are used as a laxative.*

## MAD/CRAZY

– **to be as crazy as a loon** – total verrückt sein, einen Sprung in der Schüssel haben.

I was rather worried about letting my sister go to that psychiatrist. He seemed **as crazy as a loon** himself.

– **to love someone like mad** – jemanden wahnsinnig/wie verrückt lieben.

Yvette came home in very high spirits. Her boyfriend had kissed her for the first time and she **loved him like mad**.

– **as mad as a hatter** – total verrückt/ausgeflippt.

My uncle is an artist and he's **as mad as a hatter**, but I love him very much. cf. as crazy as a coot.

– **to be like the Mad Hatter's tea-party** – *etwa:* zugehen wie in einem Tollhaus.

"When all my actor friends visited me, it was a bit **like the Mad Hatter's tea-party**".

as mad as a March Hare

cf. as mad as a March Hare. *An Austrialian variation:* **as mad as a gum tree full of galahs**.

– **as mad as a March Hare** – völlig unberechenbar/verrückt.

"My uncle lives in an antique gypsy caravan in the middle of a moor. He's **as mad as a March Hare**." cf. as mad as a hatter; as nutty as a fruitcake. *From the erratic behaviour of a marsh hare which changes direction many times on the open marsh to outwit its predators.*

## MADMAN

– **to behave/laugh/drive like a madman** – sich wie ein Verrückter benehmen/wie ein Verrückter lachen/fahren.

The drug addict was throwing rubbish all over himself and **laughing like a madman.**

The young man was said to have been **driving like a madman** before losing control of his car, mounting a pavement and hitting the wall. cf. drive like a lunatic; drive like the devil/like Jehu.

## LUNATIC

– **to behave like a raving lunatic/drive/grin like a lunatic/grin like a loon** – sich wie ein Verrückter benehmen, total ausgerastet sein/wie eine gesengte Sau fahren/grinsen wie ein Bekloppter.

**Grinning like a lunatic** and staggering about, the drunk asked the train passengers for some money.

"Don't cross the road here, Mrs Meek. You know those local lads **drive like lunatics** and can't stop so quickly."
cf. drive like a madman/like the devil. *A variation:* **to drive like Jehu**.

– **to sound like a loony idea** – wie eine verrückte/irre/unsinnige Idee/verrückt klingen.

An attempt to find a standard trouser for all three branches of the services may prove impossible. "There are not even two regiments in the British army with the same uniform. **This sounds like a loony idea**." (Mr MacKenzie, Daily Mail, 4.11.1994.)

*Variations of this simile are:* **to sound like a mad idea; like an idiotic idea; like a silly/stupid/foolish idea,** etc.; *and the opposite:* **to sound like a good/brilliant/fantastic idea,** etc.

## NERVOUS

– **to feel like a nervous wreck** – sich wie ein nervliches Wrack/ wie ein nasser Sack fühlen.

"**I feel like a nervous wreck** after looking after Sheila's children." cf. to feel like a wet rag/a washed-out rag/a bit of chewed string; to look/feel like death/like death warmed up.

## POSSESSED

– **like a man possessed/obsessed** – wie ein Besessener/Verrückter.

"**Like a man possessed**, he tried to fit the Sound Blaster Card into his computer."

"The seeds of my eventual downfall were probably already sown but I carried on **like a man obsessed**, knowing I was probably the only person who could keep father's business alive." (Major Major by Terry Major-Ball, 1994.)

## DRUG

– **like a drug** – wie eine Droge.

"There have been times when I've thought I should get out of the business. But it's **like a drug**. You get involved very easily and then it's hard to kick the habit." (Sixties pop star Billy J. Kramer, Daily Mail, 30.11.1993.)

## 13. Relations – *Menschliche Beziehungen*

### MAN

– **to fight like a man** – kämpfen wie ein Mann.

The pirate, Calico Jack was taken off to the gallows with the female pirate, Anne Bonny still rebuking him. If he had **fought like a man**, she said, he need not have been **hanged like a dog**. (Dermot Purgavie, Daily Mail, 7.12.1993.) cf. fight like a tiger/tigress; fight like a wild cat.

– **like a drowning man clutching at a straw** – wie ein Ertrinkender, der nach jedem Strohhalm greift. *From the proverb "A drowning man will clutch at a straw".*

"Your divorced wife really won't help you at all, Roy. You are **like a drowning man clutching at a straw**."
*A variation:* **like a drowning man clutching at a razor blade.**

### VIRGIN

– to achieve something **like a virgin comes to a child** – zu etwas kommen wie die Jungfrau zum Kinde.

He came to his wealth **like a virgin comes to a child**.

### FAMILY

– **like one big family/like a family** – wie eine große Familie/wie eine Familie.

"Although they were all brought up completely differently, now my sister's family, my children and stepsons get on so well it's **like one big family**. That gives me greater happiness than almost anything else in life." (Lady Sonia Melchett, a writer, Daily Mail, 23.11.1993.)

## FATHER

– **Like father, like son; like mother, like daughter** – der Apfel fällt nicht weit vom Stamm; wie der Vater so der Sohn; wie die Mutter so die Tochter.

"I told you John would end up being a book-worm like Tom. **Like father, like son**!"

## MOTHER

– **just like mother makes/just like mother used to make** – wie von Muttern gemacht.

"These cakes are really delicious – just **like mother makes**."

– **Like motherhood, we are all for it** – wir sind alle dafür; etwas Unstrittiges, Offensichtliches unterstützen.

"I'm in favour of a fair and just society", the politician told his audience. **"Like motherhood, we are all for it"**, someone shouted back.

## BABY

– **to sleep like a babe/baby** – den Schlaf der Gerechten schlafen; tief und fest schlafen wie ein Baby/wie ein Murmeltier.

"I didn't have the heart to wake Samantha up. She **was sleeping like a babe**."

On his visit to Los Angeles, Prince Charles stayed four nights at the Hotel Bel Air and found his bed in the presidential suite (yours for $ 2,000 a night) so comfortable that, according to the hotel's manager, he **slept like a baby**. (Daily Mail, 11.11.1994.)

– **as innocent as a baby** – unschuldig/naiv wie ein Baby.

"Make sure you don't walk past the red-light district with her. She's still **as innocent as a baby**." NB. *the idiom:* blue-eyed.

– **to be/behave like a baby** – sich benehmen/verhalten wie ein Baby; babyhaft.

“Can’t you stop crying and being so difficult!” the mother said sharply. “You’re just **like a baby** today!”

## CHILD

– **to act/behave like a child** – sich kindisch/wie ein Kind verhalten/benehmen.

“Just because the neighbours have bought themselves a brand new Jaguar there is no need for you to be jealous and sulk about. You’re **behaving like a child**.”

– **child-like** – unschuldig wie ein Kind; kindlich.

Mr Peterson was able to realise his **child-like** dream this year by putting up a thousand Christmas lights outside his house and in his garden.

The actor’s **child-like** innocence helped him to become famous but did nothing for his financial situation.

Linda’s **child-like** charm enabled her to have many friends.

– **as curious as a child** – neugierig wie ein Kind.

The museum in New York was quite overwhelming, and the elderly man looked around, **as curious as a child**.

## UNCLE

– **to talk to someone like a Dutch uncle** – mit jemandem Tacheles/Klartext reden; jemandem eine Standpauke halten.

“The teacher noticed that his pupil had dirty hands and **talked to him like a Dutch uncle** about being more hygienic.”

# 14. The House – *Das Haus*

## HOUSE

– **as big as a house** – riesig/riesengroß.

The little child was amazed to see the monsters in Crystal Palace Park. There were so many of them, and each **as big as a house**.

– **to get on like a house on fire** – sich blind verstehen; gut miteinander harmonieren.

"Our daughter, Diana, has never been any trouble and we've always **got on like a house on fire**."

– **to fall/collapse like a house of cards/a row of dominos** – wie ein Kartenhaus in sich zusammenfallen/einstürzen.

If Robert fails to get his university degree, all his father's plans for his future will **collapse like a house of cards**.

– **to look like the side of a house** – dick wie eine Tonne sein.

"Did you eat all my chocolates? You'll end up **looking like the side of a house**!"

– **to be as safe as houses/the bank** – in sicheren Händen/so sicher wie auf der Bank sein.

"Your money will be **as safe as houses** in that company. It's well managed and it has huge assets".

## HOME

– **no place like home** – nirgendwo ist es so schön wie zu Hause/wie am heimischen Herd; trautes Heim Glück allein; nichts geht über das Zuhause.

It's all most enjoyable here on a sunny beach in winter – but there's **no place like home** at Christmas time.

## CHURCH

– **a church-like stillness** – eine Stille wie in der Kirche.

It was nearly closing time and the museum had **a church-like stillness** about it.

## FACTORY

– **to smell like a perfume factory** – wie ein Parfümladen riechen/duften/stinken.

"I just can't walk behind that woman. She **smells like a perfume factory**!" cf. to smell like flowers/like a sewer.

## PRISON

– **like a prison/like being in a prison** – (sich vorkommen/fühlen) wie in einem Gefängnis.

"I didn't like the look of that university college. With its dark walls and small windows it was **like a prison**.

## DRAIN

– **to laugh like a drain** – sich ausschütten vor Lachen.

The English teacher had a fine sense of humour and often **laughed like a drain** in front of his students. cf. laugh like a jelly/hyena. *A variation:* **to laugh like gurgling water**.

– **drainpipe-thin** – dünn wie eine Bohnenstange, spindeldürr.

"The model was **drainpipe-thin** and very pale." cf. stick-thin; to look like a stick insect; as thin as a rake; whip-thin.

## CESSPOOL/SEWER

– **to have a mind like a cesspool/to have a mind like a sewer** – eine schmutzige/schweinische Phantasie haben.

"You should be ashamed of yourself. Your **mind is like a sewer**!"

– **to smell like a sewer** – stinken wie die Pest.

The prison cell was small and damp and **smelt like a sewer**. cf. to smell like flowers; to smell like a perfume factory.

## FURNACE/OVEN/GRIDDLE

– **as hot as a furnace/an oven/a griddle** – kochendheiß/siedendheiß.

“Stop! Don’t touch that machine! It’s **as hot as a furnace**.”

The boys had great fun frying eggs on their car bonnet. It was **as hot as an oven**. cf. as hot as fire.

## CHIMNEY

– **to smoke like a chimney** – rauchen/qualmen wie ein Schlot.

“I can’t bear the smell of smoke in here. Must you always **smoke like a chimney**?” cf. to smoke like crazy.

## BRICK

– **like talking to a brick wall** – als ob man gegen eine Wand redet.

“He thinks he knows everything better; it’s **like talking to a brick wall** arguing with him.” cf. like water off a duck’s back.

– **to come down on someone like a ton of bricks** – jemanden niedermachen/fertigmachen.

“If Brian catches you reading his diary, he’ll **come down on you like a ton of bricks**.”

## BELL

– **as clear as a bell/a voice like a little bell** – hell/deutlich/klar wie eine Glocke/glockenhell.

“Now we’ve got a new telephone I can hear you **as clear as a bell**.” cf. as clear as crystal; a voice as soft as a prayer/as syrup/as cold as steel/like an angel/like gravel/sandpaper.

like talking to a brick wall

– **to be as sound as a bell** – kerngesund sein.

“You may go back to work tomorrow, Mr Gare”, the doctor said. “I’m glad to say you’re **as sound as a bell**.” cf. fit as a fiddle.

– **like the clappers** – blitzschnell, mit affenartiger Geschwindigkeit/mit einem Affenzahn.

“The shop assistant ran **like the clappers** after the shop lifter and caught him.” cf. like a bat out of hell; like a flash of lightning.

# 15. Furniture and Household – *Möbel und Haushalt*

## LIGHT

– **to go out like a light** – zusammenbrechen wie vom Schlag/Blitz getroffen; auf der Stelle einschlafen.

After spending the whole afternoon ice-skating, the little girl **went out like a light** at bed-time.

Mary's absent-minded father banged his head on the low attic ceiling and **went out like a light**.

## CANDLE

– **as straight as a candle** – kerzengerade.

On hearing the strange noise, the dog's ears stood up **as straight as candles** and he gave a low growl. cf. as straight as a ruler.

## MIRROR

– **as smooth as a mirror/like a mirror** – spiegelglatt.

The sea (lake/pond) was **as smooth as a mirror**.

The curtain of fog is breaking ... it reveals amid the clouds a lake of air **as smooth and clear as a mirror**, the deep round eye of a white hurricane. (Winter's Tale by Mark Helprin, 1983.)

– **as polished as mirrors** – blank wie ein Spiegel, spiegelblank.

Looking through the windows of the garage one could see five or six impressive looking limousines, each **as polished as mirrors**.

## STATUE

– **as still/motionless as a statue/a post/statue-still** – wie versteinert.

A large white cat lay **as still as a statue** on top of the piano.

– **to stand like statues** – zur Salzsäule erstarrt sein.

A group of people came to look at the crater the bomb had left. They **stood like statues**, staring at it in silence.

## PICTURE

– **as pretty as a picture** – bildschön/bildhübsch.

"Emily is **as pretty as a picture**. No wonder Christopher fell in love with her."

– **picture-perfect** – wie aus dem Bilderbuch.

The trouble is, we all want Christmas to be **picture-perfect** and will go to crazy lengths to achieve it. What we fail to see is that all this effort and anticipation actually adds to the tension and makes Christmas less likely to be the way we want it. (Maeve Haran, a best selling writer, Daily Mail, 9.12.1994.)

## CARPET

– **like a magic carpet** – wie ein fliegender Teppich.

"Flying on Concorde from London to New York was **like being on a magic carpet**."

## CURTAIN

– **it looks like curtains for someone** – es sieht aus, als sei jemand weg vom Fenster/als sei der Ofen aus für jemanden.

Most of the MPs were against the Minister and **it looked like curtains** for his privatisation scheme.

## SHEET

– **as white as a sheet** – weiß wie ein Bettlaken/kreidebleich.

"Have you seen a burglar? Your face is **as white as sheet**." cf. as white as a ghost; to look like a ghost.

to look like curtains for s.o.

## BLANKET

– **like a blanket** – wie eine Decke.

The snow covered the flower-beds **like a blanket**, protecting the plants from the frost.

On bad days in Mexico City, the smog hangs in the air **like a grey, clammy blanket**. (James Fergusson, The European, 19.8.1993.)

People were very kind to us. I felt their kindness **like a blanket**, wrapping us round. (Mrs de Winter by Susan Hill, 1993.)

## NEEDLE

– **as sharp as a needle/needle-sharp** – messerscharf; äußerst präzise.

“Be well prepared when you argue with him. His mind is **as sharp as a needle**.” cf. as sharp as a razor; as sharp as a tack.

Told with **needle-sharp** accuracy for dialogue and setting. (The Good Book Guide 1994 reviewing Skylark's Song by Roy Hattersley.)

– **needle-like** – spitz/scharf wie Nadeln.

"We were enjoying the beautiful scenery when a sudden **needle--like** downpour made us run for cover."

– **like looking for a needle in a haystack** – als ob man nach einer Nadel im Heuhaufen suchen würde.

"Trying to find an aristocrat without syphilis before the French Revolution was **like looking for a needle in a haystack**." (The Fourth Horseman by Andrew Nikiforuk, 1992.)

## HAIRPIN

– **a hairpin bend** – eine Haarnadelkurve.

The tourist closed her eyes in horror when she saw another **hairpin bend** ahead of them.

## RAZOR

– **as sharp as a razor, razor-sharp** – scharf wie eine Rasierklinge/ein Messer; messerscharf.

"The game of scrabble went on for hours. Both players had minds **as sharp as razors**."

The monster's **teeth were as sharp as razors**. cf. as sharp as a needle; as sharp as a tack; NB. *the idiom:* razor-tongued.

## SPONGE

– **to soak something up like a sponge** – etwas wie ein Schwamm aufsaugen.

"Caterina is **like a sponge, soaking up knowledge**. Now that she is older, I haven't been able to keep up with it. With this lack of stimulation, she has become defiant." (Caterina's mother, Jacqui Narvaez-Jimenez, talking to Charles Hymas on why gifted children are often disadvantaged. The Sunday Times, Style and Travel, 3.10.1993.) NB. *the idiom:* a sponger – *a parasite, someone who lives at another's expense.*

## GLASS

– **as brittle as glass** – zerbrechlich wie Glas.

"Don't go near that statue, Robert. It's **as brittle as glass**."

– **as smooth as glass** – glatt wie ein Spiegel, spiegelglatt.

"The lake looked **as smooth as glass** in the early morning sunshine." cf. as smooth as a mirror.

– **the water is like glass** – das Wasser ist kristallklar.

In the early hours of this morning, the **water was like glass** and I could see the sea-bed very clearly.

– **as transparent as glass** – durchsichtig/durchscheinend wie Glas.

"At the back of the lounge was a guy as big as Arnold Schwarzenegger. His arms seemed as large as tree trunks. His face looked as if it had been cast in cement, and he had grey eyes almost **as transparent as glass**." (Watchers by Dean Koontz, 1987.)

## CRYSTAL

– **as clear as crystal/crystal-clear** – kristallklar; absolut klar und eindeutig.

"I thought I had made it **crystal-clear** that none of your boyfriends are allowed in my guest-house."

The children had great fun swimming in the **crystal-clear waters** of the Aegean Sea. cf. *the opposite:* as clear as mud.

## CHALICE

– **like a poisoned chalice** – wie ein vergifteter Kelch/ein Gifttrunk.

The General was given the command of the peace-keeping army but everyone knew it was **like a poisoned chalice** for him in that war-torn country. cf. to hate someone like poison.

## KNIFE

– **like a knife through butter** – wie ein Messer durch die Butter.

The hurricane wreaked enormous damage. In one village a tree went through a house **like a knife through butter**.

– **the wind cuts into/through someone like a knife/like a thousand knives** – ein schneidend kalter Wind durchdringt jemanden.

The spy waited for the secret agent next to the dyke facing the sea, and the **icy wind cut through him like a knife**.

## PORCELAIN

– **skin like porcelain** – Haut wie aus Porzellan/Porzellanhaut.

"We need a model with **skin like porcelain** to advertise our new face cream", the agent said, looking hopefully at all the girls' faces.

## SAUCER

– **eyes as big as saucers** – riesengroße Augen.

"We shall always remember that llama", the mother laughed. "It's **eyes were as big as saucers**." cf. eyes like golf balls.
*A variation:* **eyes as big as plates**.

## SIEVE

– **to have a memory like a sieve/to have a head like a sieve** – ein Gedächtnis wie ein Sieb haben.

"When it comes to people's names, I **have a memory like a sieve**." cf. *the opposite:* to have a memory like an elephant.

## BRUSH

– **as daft as a brush** – dumm wie Bohnenstroh.

"You must be **as daft as a brush** to have given your beautiful map to that tourist. You'll never see it again."

## STRING

– **to feel like a bit of chewed string** – sich fühlen wie durch die Mangel gedreht.

After cooking for so many unexpected guests, the cook groaned: "I **feel like a bit of chewed string**." cf. to feel like a wet rag.

## RECORD

– **to repeat like a cracked record/to sound like a record stuck in a groove** – sich wiederholen/klingen wie eine gesprungene Schallplatte.

When her husband, Mick, confronted the doctor about why he had continued with the operation, "he just kept **repeating like a cracked record** that it was because of her age, that she had two stepsons and had suffered from depression." (The European, 12.9.1993.)

# 16. Food – *Nahrung*

## MILK

– **as white as milk/milk-white** – schneeweiß.

A Riddle by Robert Herrik:

In marble walls **as white as milk**,
lined with a **skin as soft as silk**;
Within a fountain crystal clear
A golden apple doth appear.
No doors there are to this stronghold,
Yet thieves break in and steal the gold. (*Answer:* an egg.)

cf. as white as snow/as a lily; pearl-white; to look as white as a ghost/a sheet; NB. *the adjective:* milky-white.

## CHEESE

– **to be like/as different as chalk and cheese** – unterschiedlich/verschieden wie Tag und Nacht sein.

"You'd never think that Paul and Sue were twins. They are **as different as chalk and cheese**."

The two sisters were **like chalk and cheese** but they lived very happily together in their little country cottage.

cf. like day and night.

## EGG

– **like the curate's egg** – *etwa:* sich schönfärberisch zu etwas keineswegs Lobenswertem ausdrücken; es ist streckenweise gar nicht so schlecht.

"What did you think of the Minister's speech?" "It was **like the curate's egg**."

– **as sure/simple as eggs is eggs** – so sicher wie das Amen in der Kirche; so sicher wie 1 plus 1 gleich zwei ist.

It's like swimming through porridge.

"My husband has mislaid the theatre tickets and you can be **as sure as eggs is eggs** that he will say it is my fault!" *The mathematical 'x is x' sounds quite similar to 'eggs is eggs'.* cf. as sure as hell.

## EGGSHELL

– **like walking on egg-shells** – als ob man mit einem rohen Ei umgeht.

"There's an important business deal coming up and my boss is very tense and short-tempered. **It's like walking on egg-shells** working for him today." cf. *the idiom:* to tread upon eggs.

## BUTTER

– **as soft as butter** – weich wie Butter/butterweich; verweichlicht.

"The little boy stepped onto the newly cemented driveway but to his surprise the cement was still **as soft as butter**."

If anyone was ever branded by the company she kept, my first wife certainly was – her women friends were **as hard as nails** and **as tough as old boots**, and her men friends were **as soft as butter** and **as limp as last week's lettuce**. (The Ladies of Missalonghi by Colleen McCullough, 1987.)

## BREAD

– **something is like bread without butter** – etwas ist wie eine Suppe ohne Salz.

"Eurovision without Terry Wogan is **like bread without butter**." (A spokesman for Tim Rice, defending Terry Wogan's role as presenter of the Eurovision Song Contest. Daily Mail, 2.6.1994.)
cf. like Hamlet without the Prince.

## TOAST

– **as warm as toast** – *etwa:* wohlig warm.

Jessica felt **as warm as toast** after her hot bubble bath.

## PORRIDGE

– **to be like swimming through porridge/corn syrup** – *etwa:* eine mühsame Arbeit sein.

"Trying to understand the complicated treaty was **like swimming through porridge** for the politicians." cf. like thinking through treacle. *A variation:* **like swimming through jelly with both hands tied behind one's back.**

## HONEY

– **as sweet as honey** – süß wie Honig; honigsüß; zuckersüß.

"The girls were **as sweet as honey** as long as I did what they wanted." *A variation:* **to be as sweet as pie**.

## SYRUP

– **a voice as smooth as syrup** – eine einschmeichelnde/seidenweiche Stimme.

"The film star was tall and handsome, and his **voice was as smooth as syrup**." NB. *the idiom:* soothing syrup; cf. a voice as cold as steel; a voice like an angel/like a little bell; a voice as soft as a prayer.

## TREACLE

– **to be like thinking through treacle** – keinen klaren Gedanken mehr fassen können.

After drinking too much at the party and coming home too late, Martin had trouble with his Latin test the following morning. **"It was like thinking through treacle**", he later told his friends.
cf. like swimming through porridge/corn syrup/jelly.

## CHOCOLATE

– **as useless as a chocolate kettle** – zu nichts nütze; absolut nutzlos.

"Don't just stand there! Do something! You're **as useless as a chocolate kettle**."

– **chocolate-box image** – Postkartenimage.

Cornish piskies, mackerel fishing trips and clotted-cream teas are out. Stark, granite quarries, wave-smashed shingle and wind-ravaged trees are in. The pretty **chocolate-box image** of Cornwall is a cliché. (Spoken by Ferdinand Fairfax, television director of the detective series Wycliffe. Daily Mail, 30. 7. 1994.)

## TOFFEE

– **to dole something out like toffees** – etwas wie Bonbons/freigiebig austeilen.

Doctors should stop **doling** anti-depressants **out like toffees.**

## JELLY

– **to shake, tremble, quiver like a jelly** – zittern wie Espenlaub.

Charlotte was **trembling like a jelly** whilst waiting for her exam results. cf. to tremble/shake like a leaf; legs like jelly.

– **to laugh like a jelly** – beben vor Lachen.

"Wait till he gets you in the swimming pool," Ma said and, **laughing like a jelly**, went away to put the pheasants into the oven and little Oscar into bed. (From When the Green Woods Laugh by H. E. Bates, 1960.) cf. laugh like a drain/gurgling water/hyena.

– **like trying to nail jelly to a wall** – *etwa:* ein Ding der Unmöglichkeit.

"Trying to make those two enemy countries stick to any agreement is **like trying to nail jelly to a wall**." cf. as easy as juggling with soot.

## BLANCMANGE

– **legs like blancmange/like jelly** – Beine wie Pudding/Pudding in den Beinen.

The plump bank manager couldn't cycle up the steep hill. His **legs were like blancmange.**

## CAKES

– **to sell/go like hot cakes** – weggehen wie warme Semmeln.

Even if tales about dragons and princes and people with funny names are not exactly your cup of tea, it has to be acknowledged that fantasy fiction now **sells like hot cakes**." (Val Hennessy, Daily Mail, 13.9.1993.) cf. to go like a bomb.

## FRUITCAKE

– **to be as nutty as a fruitcake** – eine Schraube locker haben.

Jamie loved fooling about at school and all his friends thought he was as **nutty as a fruitcake**. cf. as mad as a hatter, as mad as a March Hare. *Nutty is one of many English expressions for insane or mad such as: to be off one's nut; to be nuts; to be a nut-case; to be nuts about someone.*

## PANCAKE

– **one's chest is as flat as a pancake** – flach wie ein Brett sein.

"You can't wear that low-cut dress. Your **chest is as flat as a pancake**!" cf. as curvaceous as an ice-pop; to knock someone down as flat as a flounder.
*A variation:* **one's hair is as flat as a pancake.**

– **to fall as flat as a pancake** – ins Leere gehen, verpuffen.

"The joke **fell as flat as a pancake**; nobody laughed."

## PASTRY

– **as pale as pastry** – leichenblaß/wie eine lebende Leiche.

Jane was in bed with flu and looked **as pale as pastry**. cf. as pale as death, as white as a sheet/chalk.

## PIE

– **to be as sweet as pie** – süß wie Honig/zuckersüß sein.

"She could be **as sweet as pie** if she wanted to get something out of me." cf. to be as sweet as honey.

– **as easy as pie** – kinderleicht.

Learning to cook these vegetarian dishes is **as easy as pie**.
cf. as easy as ABC/as winking/as falling off a log/as shelling peas.

## WAFER

– **wafer-thin** – hauchdünn.

Computer projections suggested that Chancellor Helmut Kohl's coalition would hold on to power by a **wafer-thin** majority. (Daily Mail, 17.10.1994.) cf. paper-thin; stick-thin, drainpipe-thin, as thin as a rake; gossamer-thin.

## MUTTON

– **to look like mutton dressed as lamb** – wie eine aufgetakelte alte Schachtel/Fregatte aussehen.

"That old film star really shouldn't wear such a short dress. She looks **like mutton dressed as lamb**." cf. *the opposite:* like a spring chicken.

## BACON & EGGS

– **to go together like bacon and eggs** – zusammenpassen wie die Faust aufs Auge/wie ein Paar alte Latschen.

"British Rail and safety are **like bacon and eggs**." (Robert Adley, Tory M.P. for Christchurch on Radio 4, 13.12.1988.)

## MUSTARD

– **as keen as mustard** – verrückt/versessen auf, Feuer und Flamme für.

The millionaire bought the whole holiday camp and he was **as keen as mustard** to buy the local supermarket as well.

## VINEGAR

– **as sour as vinegar** – sauer wie eine unreife Zitrone, eine beleidigte Leberwurst.

"Emma cut the cloth all wrong by mistake and now Katie is **as sour as vinegar**." cf. as sour as limes.

## LIME

– **lime-green** – limonengrün.

The punk had dyed his hair **lime-green**, white and orange so as to make a big impression on the photographer. cf. pea-green.

## ORANGE

– **to discard someone like a sucked orange** – jemanden fallenlassen wie eine heiße Kartoffel; der Mohr hat seine Pflicht getan, der Mohr kann gehen.

After working in the same firm for ten years, Roger was **discarded like a sucked orange**.

– **as round as an orange** – groß wie eine Orange.

"The wasp sting was swelling up very rapidly on Daniel's leg and soon it was **as round as an orange**."

## APPLE

– **to fall to someone like a ripe apple** – jemandem wie eine reife Frucht in den Schoß fallen.

"Independence will **fall to us** one day **like a ripe apple**." (Gandhi talking about India gaining its independence from Great Britain.)

## PEACH

– **to have skin like a peach** – pfirsichzarte Haut/Pfirsichhaut haben.

"That girl who advertises soap on television has got **skin like a peach**." cf. skin as soft as milk/as white as snow; skin like porcelain; a china-doll complexion.

## PRUNES

– **facts, dates,** etc. **go through one like prunes** – Fakten, Daten *usw.* gehen zum einen Ohr hinein, zum anderen Ohr hinaus.

"In Cordoba, our guide told us stories and regaled us with history, but **dates** I'm afraid **go through me like prunes**." (Neil Maclean, Daily Mail, 30.7.1994.) *Prunes, soaked in water, are a very effective laxative.*

## NUTS

– **as crinkled/wrinkled as a walnut/wrinkled like a walnut** – verschrumpelt wie ein getrockneter Apfel.

The old farmer's face was as **crinkled as a walnut**, from being out in the sun all day.

The human brain is an object weighing, on average, just over two pounds, **wrinkled like a walnut**, with the colour and something of the consistency of porridge. (The Making of Memory by Steven Rose, 1993.)

An alcoholic's liver is **like a pickled walnut**.

– **as brown as a walnut** – nußbraun.

**Brown as a walnut** and **lined like wrinkled linen,** 70-year old Alice lives in a farmhouse called Roseledge. (A book review of Alice's Masque by Lindsay Clarke, Daily Mail, 22.1.1994.) cf. as brown as a berry.

– **eyes like almonds/almond-like eyes** – mandelförmige Augen.

Mambi was a very attractive girl with **eyes like almonds** and long, shining black hair.

## VEGETABLE/CABBAGE

– **to become like a vegetable/cabbage** – *etwa:* dahinvegetieren.

"We don't fear death: the process of dying is something that we have discussed. Roy said that if it was a question of him **becoming like a vegetable** through some illness or other, that would be much worse than dying suddenly." (Roy Castle's wife, Fiona. Daily Mail, 27.11.1993.)

"**I was like a cabbage** for days after the accident. I'm so glad I'm well again."

## BEAN

– **to look like a string bean** – wie eine Bohnenstange aussehen.

"John never became fat in his middle age and he still **looks like a string bean**." cf. as thin as a rake; to grow like a beanstalk.

## PEAS

– **to be as like as two peas** – sich wie ein Ei dem anderen gleichen; jemandem wie aus dem Gesicht geschnitten sein.

"The twin boys are **as like as two peas**." *Variations:* **as like as two eggs; as like as two book-ends; as like as two herrings.**

– **as easy as shelling peas** – kinderleicht.

"They told me at the travel agency that finding our way from the airport to the hotel is **as easy as shelling peas**." cf. as easy as falling off a log/as ABC/as winking/as pie.

## CARROT

– **like a carrot to a donkey** – wie ein Köder.

"Would you have gone with that bank robber if he had dangled the plane ticket in front of your nose, **like a carrot to a donkey**?" *A stick to a donkey means a threat.* NB. *the idiom:* the stick and carrot policy.

## POTATO

– **to drop someone/something like a hot potato** – etwas/jemanden wie eine heiße Kartoffel fallen lassen.

When Rebecca found out that her boyfriend took drugs, she **dropped him like a hot potato**.

– **to be thrown like a hot potato** – *etwa*: von Pontius zu Pilatus geschickt werden.

"It makes no difference how many times and how many ways I try to explain my case. For the last two dreadful years I have been

like a couch potato

**thrown like a hot potato** from one organisation to another. (Romanian asylum-seeker No. 26050520. The European, 26.2.1992.)

– **like a couch potato** – wie jemand, der nur faul ist und ständig vor der Glotze hockt.

As the surgeons point out, unless you go crazy with over-eating and live **like a couch potato**, once the fat has gone, it won't come back. Unlike diets, liposuction could be for ever. (Jane Alexander reporting on the latest tactic to beat cellulite. Daily Mail, 22.1.1994.)

## LETTUCE

– **as limp as last week's lettuce** – schlapp wie ein nasser Sack.

Her men friends were as soft as butter and **as limp as last week's lettuce**. (The Ladies of Missalonghi by Colleen McCullough, 1987.)

## CUCUMBER

– **as cool as a cucumber** – kalt wie eine Hundeschnauze; kaltblütig.

"Prince Charles was **as cool as a cucumber** after the attempt to assassinate him in Sydney." *A Variation:* as cool as an iceberg.

## POISON

– **to hate someone like poison** – jemanden hassen wie die Pest.

The young man **hated his neighbour like poison** after he complained about his loud music. cf. like a poisoned chalice.

## WINE

– **like wine/to keep like a good wine** – wie ein guter Wein/haltbar sein und reifen wie ein guter Wein. *A good wine tastes better with age.*

The magazine argues that the luckiest women are the "ugly ducklings" who bloomed with maturity, **keeping like a good wine**, working on their feminine arts without the superficial, transitory distraction of overt good looks. (Jane Kelly, Daily Mail, 21.9.1993.)

**Perfumes are like wine:** some get even better with age. (Jean Kerleo, Daily Mail, 9.12.1993.)

## BARREL

– **as round as a barrel** – rund wie eine Kugel/Faß; kugelrund.

"After drinking 5 litres of beer, Jack's stomach was **as round as a barrel**."

# 17. Clothes – *Kleidung*

## SHOES

– **as comfortable as an old shoe** – bequem, entspannt, unkompliziert und aufgeschlossen.

The ill patient was relieved to find that his nurse was **as comfortable as an old shoe**. *An American simile.*

– **to be as common as an old shoe** – aufgeschlossen, natürlich und freundlich sein; keine Allüren haben; auf dem Boden/Teppich bleiben. *An American simile.*

The university professor had written many highly praised books but he was still **as common as an old shoe** to his fellow lecturers.

– **as welcome as water in one's shoes** – *etwa:* vollkommen unerwünscht/absolut nicht willkommen.

To our horror our visitor had chicken pox and was **as welcome as water in our shoes**. cf. *the opposite:* as welcome as flowers in May.

– **like waiting for a dead man's shoes** – als ob man darauf wartet, daß jemand stirbt, damit man seine Stelle bekommt.

The ambitious assistant manager, Mr Green, soon realised that waiting for a full managerial position was **like waiting for dead men's shoes** and decided to start a business of his own.

## BOOTS

– **as tough/hard as old boots** – zäh wie Leder/hart wie Stein.

Mrs Croxted looks so frail and helpless but when you start doing business with her you'll find she is **as tough as old boots**.

"You are so absent-minded! You forgot to put the bread into the bread bin and now it is **as hard as old boots**."

as tough/hard as old boots

"I'm never going to buy frozen beef from that shop again. I thought I cooked it well but it's **as tough as old boots**." cf. as hard/tough as nails; as tough as leather.

– **to work like old boots** – arbeiten wie ein Pferd/sehr energisch und zielstrebig handeln. *An American simile.*

The road sweeper was **working like old boots** to get the road clean for the Royal Procession.

## TOE-RAG

– **to treat someone like a toe-rag/like toe-rags** – jemanden wie den letzten Dreck behandeln.

"Whyever do you still want to work for that man when he **treats you like a toe-rag**?" cf. treat like dirt/a leper; treat like animals.

## GLOVE

– **to fit like a glove** – wie angegossen passen; passen wie die Faust aufs Auge.

She looks very elegant in her trouser-suit. It **fits** her **like a glove**.

The description given by the policeman on Crime Watch **fitted** the suspect **like a glove**. cf. to fit like a second skin.

## BUTTON

– **as bright/cute as a button** – ein helles Licht; intelligent und aufgeweckt.

"Robin will pass his spelling test easily. He's **as bright as a button**."

## BANDBOX

– **bandbox fresh/fresh as a bandbox/bandbox neat** – wie aus dem Ei gepellt.

Princess Diana was never less than **bandbox fresh**, an everlasting bright candle in a dark and dismal world. Her clothes were chosen with taste and worn with enviable skill. She looked exactly what she ought to be: a princess of England. (Paul Johnson, Daily Mail, 4.12.1993.)

## BAG

– **to look like an old bag** – wie eine Schreckschraube aussehen.

"At home I do my best to look smart and well-groomed. My sons don't want me to **look like an old bag**".

– **to look like a bag-lady** – wie eine Stadtstreicherin aussehen.

Miss Kate Adie, who has just returned from Bosnia, confesses that she came home from covering the brutal civil war **looking like a bag lady**. "It's no good **looking like a ratbag**, although I always hit civilisation as the only dirty person in Vienna airport." (BBC's Kate Adie, Daily Mail, 11.8.1993.)

## SACK

– **dress like a sack/as shapeless as a sack** – unförmig aussehen wie in einem Sack.

The traveller was wearing a dull grey dress which was **as shapeless as a sack**. *A rude variation:* **to look like a sack of potatoes**.

## RAG

– **to feel like a wet rag/feel/look like a washed-out rag** – sich wie ein nasser Sack/ausgelaugt fühlen.

"Thank goodness the school holidays are over tomorrow. I **feel like a washed-out rag**." cf. to feel like a nervous wreck/a bit of chewed string; to look/feel like death/like death warmed up.

## SILK

– **as soft/smooth as silk** – weich und geschmeidig wie Seide.

"Your skin is **as soft as silk**", Richard said admiringly to Miranda, gently stroking her cheek. cf. hair like silk, skin like a peach; NB. a silky voice.

"I've seen Zeppelin's first airship flying – it's as big as a city block and **as smooth as silk**." (Winter by Den Deighton, 1987.)

## VELVET/SATIN

– **as smooth as velvet/like velvet/satin** – weich wie Samt, samtweich.

"She had just washed her hair and now it was **as smooth as velvet**.

## LEATHER

– **as tough as leather** – zäh wie Leder.

"I am very surprised that such old meat is being sold. The nutritional quality will be poorer, the protein would be all right, but vitamins and iron will have deteriorated. Also the meat would probably be **as tough as leather**." (The European, 9.9.1993.) cf. as tough as old boots; as hard as a rock.

## 18. Places and Nationalities – *Städte und Länder*

### NEWCASTLE

– **like carrying coals to Newcastle** – als ob man Eulen nach Athen tragen würde.

"It would be **like carrying coals to Newcastle** if you were to give the maitre chef de cuisine a cookery book."

### ABERDEEN

– **to have a face like a wet Sunday in Aberdeen** – ein Gesicht machen wie sieben Tage Regenwetter.

The man laughed and choked at his joke and when he saw that the Queen was not laughing, he prodded her and said, "Aw, c'mon, lassie, let yourself go. You've got **a face** on you **like a wet Sunday in Aberdeen**." (The Queen and I by Sue Townsend, 1992.) cf. a face like a fiddle/as long as a fiddle; a face like thunder.

### TROJAN

– **like a Trojan horse** – wie ein Trojanisches Pferd; wie russische Puppen.

The European Commission is behaving **like a Trojan horse**, allowing the United States to subordinate our interests to theirs. (Marie-France Garaud, former French government adviser, on the GATT talks. The European, 1993.)

– **to work like a Trojan/like Trojans** – arbeiten wie ein Pferd/ Kuli.

"The workmen are **working like Trojans** so that the house will be ready by next week." cf. work like a slave/like hell/like a dog/a horse/beavers/like a dream/like magic.

## JERICHO

– **to fall like the walls of Jericho** – einstürzen/zusammenfallen wie ein Kartenhaus.

Don't worry about the court-case. His arguments **will fall like the walls of Jericho**.

## NORMAN

– **to answer like a Norman** – ausweichend antworten.

The unemployed youth asked the politician if he could help him, but he **answered like a Norman**.

## THE RED SEA

– **to part like the Red Sea/like the Red Sea parting** – sich teilen/öffnen wie das Rote Meer.

to part like the Red Sea

The rush-hour traffic **parted** for the ambulance **like the Red Sea**.

When the Prime Minister walks into a room, **it's like the Red Sea parting**.

### MEDES AND PERSIANS

– **like the laws of the Medes and the Persians** – wie ein ewigwährendes Recht.

You must surely have realised by now that you can't hope to change the school rules. They are **like the laws of the Medes and the Persians**.

### CHINESE

– **like Chinese torture/like Chinese water torture** – wie chinesische Wasserfolter, die reinste Folter.

Hearing the children's tennis balls thud, thud, thudding outside her window all day long was **like Chinese torture** for old Mrs Higgens.

Shopping is a pain, and, like all pains, is best got over with in one intense burst rather than by absorbing a little errand each day **like some sort of Chinese water torture**. (Ironing John by James Leith, 1994.)

## 19. Names – *Namen*

### ADAM

– **to be as old as Adam** – steinalt sein; einen langen Bart haben.

"That funny story is **as old as Adam**. Can't you tell us another one?" cf. as old as the hills; as old as Methuselah.

## JACOB

– **like Jacob's Ladder** – wie die/eine Jakobsleiter. *Eine Jacobsleiter ist eine Strickleiter, die an der Bordwand von Schiffen herabgelassen wird.*

To get out of the dungeon, the visitors to the castle had to climb up a very steep staircase. It looked **like Jacob's Ladder**.

## CROESUS

– **as rich as Croesus** – Geld wie Heu, reich wie Krösus.

"I really don't know what to give him for Christmas. He's **as rich as Croesus** and has everything he needs already." cf. as rich as a king.

## SOLOMON

– **as wise as Solomon** – weise wie Salomon, salomonisch.

"I'm glad he's going to become our new headmaster. He's **as wise as Solomon**." cf. as wise as an owl.

## JOB

– **as patient as Job** – geduldig wie ein Engel; Engelsgeduld.

"Katie is really good at looking after those little children. She's **as patient as Job**."

## DAVID AND JONATHAN

– **to be like David and Jonathan** – unzertrennlich sein wie siamesische Zwillinge.

Those two lads are quite inseparable. They are **like David and Jonathan**.

## MADONNA

– **a Madonna-like serenity** – madonnenhafte Gelassenheit; eine engelhafte Ausstrahlung.

Her large, gentle hazel eyes and broad cheekbones gave her face **a Madonna-like serenity,** and the freckles were fading from her complexion, leaving it **as white as porcelain**. (Night Shall Overtake Us by Kate Saunders, 1994.)

## CAESAR'S WIFE

– **like Caesar's wife** – über jeden Verdacht erhaben; überaus seriös.

Clergy husbands and wives live in the public eye and must be **like Caesar's wife**. They are expected to be the model couple and must set a good example to their parishioners.

## CANUTE

– **Canute-like** – wie jemand, der das Unvermeidliche zu verhindern sucht.

John Gummer, the environment secretary, who has, **Canute-like**, issued stern statements discouraging out-of-town sprawl, should come to Cross Point Business Park to learn an unpalatable fact: too late, chum. (Hugh Pearman examining the ugly, ecologically unsound, multi-purpose centres springing up near so many motorway junctions, The Sunday Times, 20.11.1994.)

## QUEEN ANNE

– **to be as dead as Queen Anne** – ein alter Hut sein; einen langen Bart haben.

"Did you say Michael Jackson got married? That news is **as dead as Queen Anne**. We heard all about that weeks ago!"
cf. as dead as a door-nail; as dead as a nail in a coffin; as dead as a tent-peg.

## KAFKA

– **Kafka-like** – surrealistisch, unwirklich; kafkaesk.

One of the recurrent themes in the book 'Alice in Wonderland' is constraint – characters who can only move in fixed patterns, on a chessboard or round a tea table. **Kafka-like**, the books abound in rules that must be obeyed, adult threats, unanswerable questions. They may reflect Dodgson's repressed psyche or merely his sense of the ridiculousness of adult rituals. (Peter Lewis, The Sunday Times, The Culture, 6.11.1994.)

## HOUDINI

– **Houdini-like** – wie der Entfesselungskünstler Houdini.

The corrupt politicians we saw in that film had a **Houdini-like** skill in escaping conviction.

Houdini-like

## BOOTLES' BABY

– **to look like Bootles' baby** – aufgetakelt sein wie eine Fregatte. *This simile refers only to females.*

"My goodness, Catherine! You **look like Bootles' baby**! We're only going to have tea at our neighbour's."

## LARRY

– **as happy as Larry** – sehr glücklich.

My brothers are **as happy as Larry** playing football all day. cf. as happy as a lark; as happy as a dog with two tails.

## ST ELMO

– **a grin like St Elmo's fire** – ein feines, flackerndes, verschmitztes Grinsen.

"Oh yes, it's all going our way now!" commented Lord Tebbit to me, **a grin** flickering across his lips **like St Elmo's fire**. Granny's message, let alone her own good self, can't be shovelled back into the attic yet. (Daily Mail, 8.10.1993.)

## ROLLS ROYCE

– **to move/run like a Rolls** – laufen wie am Schnürchen/wie geschmiert. *Usually said of a motor-car or of other power-driven vehicles. Rolls Royce motors are of a very superior quality.*

"Congratulations! I never thought you would be able to repair my car, but now **it moves like a Rolls**!"

# 20. Monarchy – *Monarchie*

## EMPEROR

- **Eat like an Emperor at breakfast time**, **eat like a King at lunch time**, and **eat like a beggar at dinner time** (*or* give your enemy your dinner). *An old saying* – Frühstücke wie ein Kaiser, iß wie ein König zu Mittag und wie ein Bettler zu Abend.

- **like the Emperor's new clothes** – wie des Kaisers neue Kleider/als ob man des Kaisers neue Kleider loben würde.

The $ 5,000 display of pots of cheese and jam covered in various shades of fungus was much praised by the artist's friends until a journalist said it was **like the Emperor's new clothes**.

## ROYALTY

- **to feel like royalty** – sich wie ein König/wie eine Königin fühlen.

to feel like royalty

"Their last car was an old Austrian Princess limo. My aunts used to **feel like royalty** sitting in the back." (John Herrod talking about his two aunts who are being hunted by the police in Britain and in Ireland. Daily Mail, 26. 7. 1993.)

## KING

– **as rich as a king** – steinreich/stinkreich.

"The young man's invention was so popular he soon became **as rich as a king**." c.f. as rich as Croesus.

– **to be treated like a king** – wie ein König/königlich behandelt werden.

"I expect to be **treated like a king**", was the answer the Indian prince, Porus, gave to Alexander the Great on being taken prisoner. This impressed Alexander so much that he made friends with Porus and gave him back his kingdom.

– **to feel like a king** – sich wie ein König fühlen; sich prächtig fühlen.

On leaving school, Dahl joined Shell and was sent to what is now Tanzania. He and two other young Englishmen ran Shell's business in a country four times the size of Great Britain. It made him **feel like a king**. (Roald Dahl by Jeremy Treglown, 1994.)

## QUEEN

– **to feel like a queen** – sich wie eine Königin/königlich fühlen.

"Without you I am nothing. With you, I **feel like a queen**." (From a letter Sonya wrote to her husband, Leo Tolstoy, in November 1864.) cf. to feel like a princess; to feel/look like a million dollars.

## PRINCE

– **to be waited on like a prince** – bedient werden wie ein Prinz.

During all his formative years, he was **waited on like a prince**. "I lost touch with reality. I didn't learn to do anything for myself until much later." (Ricky Schroder who acted Little Lord Fauntleroy, Daily Mail, 17.12.1992.)

## PRINCESS

– **to feel like a princess** – sich wie eine Prinzessin fühlen.

"The handsome, well-bred owner of Luckworth Hall could make any ordinary girl **feel like a princess**." cf. to feel like a queen; to feel/look like a million dollars.

## LORD

– **to live like a lord/Sultan** – wie die Made im Speck leben.

"I don't know where he gets the money from, but he seems to be **living like a lord**."

Property millionaire David Hart was born and raised in great opulence. "I **live like a Sultan**", he once said, "and money means nothing to me." (Daily Mail, 23.9.1994.)

– **as drunk as a lord** – sternhagelvoll, voll wie eine Haubitze.

"When I arrived at the party last night, your boy-friend was already **as drunk as a lord**." cf. as drunk as a fiddler; as drunk as blazes.

## LADY

– **like a lady/lady-like/in a lady-like way/manner/fashion** – wie eine Dame (von Welt)/damenhaft.

"Make sure you get out of the car **in a lady-like way**", the Duchess warned her teenage daughter. "The photographers will be waiting for you!"

## GENTLEMAN

– **to behave like a gentleman** – sich wie ein Herr/Gentleman/ Mann von Welt benehmen.

Peter **behaved like a gentleman** and held the door open for the lady.

## HISTORY

– **like holding a piece of history** – als ob man ein Stück Geschichte in der Hand hält/den Atem der Geschichte spürt.

The statue of the Maltese Falcon is expected to fetch £30,000 when it goes under the hammer at Christie's in New York. One Christie's staff member who was allowed to lift the statue said yesterday: "**It's like holding a piece of history in your hands**." (Daily Mail, 25.11.1994.)

# 21. War and Weapons – *Krieg und Waffen*

## TROOPER

– **to swear like a trooper** – fluchen wie ein Landsknecht/Bierkutscher.

The English have long been renowned as a foul-mouthed nation. "King Henry VIII and Queen Elizabeth I **swore like troopers.** (Jeffrey Richards, Professor of Cultural History at Lancaster University, Daily Mail, 28.7.1993.) cf. to swear like an ostler/a bummaree.

## CAVALRY

– **to charge in like the 7th cavalry** – *etwa:* impulsiv handeln; mit der Tür ins Haus fallen.

"If we want to catch these criminals, we must plan things carefully and not go **charging in like the 7th cavalry**."

## MILITARY OPERATION

– **like a military operation** – generalstabsmäßig.

"We've got both our parents coming for Christmas, as well as two uncles and Aunt Joe with her baby," Barbara said nervously to her husband. "We'll have to plan everything **like a military operation**."

## BOMB

– **to go like a bomb** – wie warme Semmeln weggehen; sich blitzartig fortbewegen.

"Our vegetarian cookery books **are going like a bomb** after the film star praised them on television." cf. like hot cakes.

"It was so exciting watching that new train. It **went like a bomb**!"

– **to go down like a bomb** – wie eine Bombe einschlagen.

The news that their cousin was a thief **went down like a bomb** in the family.

– **like a bombshell/to land/hit like a bombshell** – wie eine Bombe/Granate (einschlagen).

"The day my father said that he was going to take holy orders to become an Anglican vicar was **like a bombshell**". (Lady Christine Vincent, a writer and former Bunny Girl, Daily Mail, 18.8.1994.)

The paperback edition of Diana: Her True Story **landed like a bombshell** in the stores and is expected to soar to No. 1 on the best-seller list. (George Gordon, Daily Mail, 7.11.1992.)

"The revelations about the politician's past life have **hit the United States like a bombshell**."

– **like a time bomb waiting to explode/like sitting on a time bomb** – als ob man auf einer Zeitbombe/einem Vulkan sitzt.

The book landed like a bombshell in the stores.

The blackmailer put the video cassette on the director's desk, and there it lay, **like a time bomb waiting to explode**."

"Most sudden deaths for athletes are caused by hypertrophic cardiomyopathy (HCM) – excessive thickening of the heart muscle – which affects up to 10,000 people in Britain. One parent said that his daughter, Claire, carries one of the three rogue genes known to cause the condition, and that it is **like sitting on a time bomb** for them." (Daily Mail, 21.5.1994.) cf. like sitting on a volcano.

– **to sound like a bomb going off** – klingen wie eine explodierende Bombe.

It was so slippery that a lorry skidded on the ice and crashed into a shop window. The impact **sounded like a bomb going off**.
cf. a noise like thunder.

– **look like bomb-sites** – aussehen wie nach einem Bombenangriff.

The hurricane-force winds left large areas of London **looking like bomb-sites**.

## TORPEDO

– **like a torpedo** – wie ein Blitz.

The shape from the water came at Nadine Cloer **like a torpedo**, and the **razor-sharp teeth** of an 8ft barracuda closed around her. (Tony Burton, Daily Mail, 13. 7. 1993.) cf. like lightning.

## GRENADE

– **like pulling the pin from a grenade** – wie der Funke im Pulverfaß.

"If the French troops were to leave Rwanda, it would be **like pulling the pin from a grenade**."

## CANNON

– **to be like a loose cannon/like a political loose cannon** – auf dem Pulverfaß sitzen.

The Minister had so many enemies and was so rude to everyone that he was **like a political loose cannon**.

## MINEFIELD

– **like a minefield/like walking through a minefield** – eine Gratwanderung.

"Nutritional advice is so conflicting and confusing. Trying to work your way around what is good for you and what isn't is **like a minefield**." (Delia Smith, Daily Mail, 25. 5. 1993.) cf. like treading on egg-shells.

## GUN

– **as sure as a gun** – todsicher.

“If that politician promises to crack down on crime, **sure as a gun** he’ll win lots of votes.” c.f. as sure as eggs is eggs; as sure as hell.

– **to rain like a son of a gun** – regnen wie aus Kübeln; in Strömen gießen. *An American simile.*

Lou Chiodini of the Army Corps of Engineers said: “It’s **raining like a son of a gun** right now.” Midwest, USA which experienced the greatest flood America has known. (Daily Mail, 22.7.1993.)

## SHOT

– **like a shot** – wie aus der Pistole geschossen; blitzschnell.

If it weren’t for my boyfriend, I’d be away from here **like a shot**.

## PIKESTAFF

– **as plain as a pikestaff** – klar wie Kloßbrühe, unmißverständlich.

“Oh no! You got the wrong jam. The label here says “For Diabetics”, **as plain as a pikestaff**.” c.f. as plain as the nose on your face. *A variation:* **as plain as murder/day**.

## RAMROD

– **as straight/stiff as a ramrod/rod** – kerzengerade, als ob man einen Besenstiel verschluckt hätte.

“No reply was forthcoming. Nothing about Matsuyama-San had visibly changed. He still sat there, **stiff as a ramrod**, a non-committal expression on his face, but there was no movement whatsoever.” (The Old Man and Mr Smith by Peter Ustinov, 1990.)

“On hearing that her son had smashed her car she was ashen-faced and **as stiff as a rod**.”

cf. as stiff as a poker/as a board; NB. a ramrod spine; NB. *the idiom:* to make a rod for one’s own back.

## SWORD

– **words/actions feel like a sword through one's heart** – Worte/ Taten treffen wie ein Stich ins Herz.

"This is the last night of freedom in your life, so make the most of it", the new bodyguard, Chief Inspector Paul Officer, told Lady Diana Spencer. "**Those words**", she would say, "**felt like a sword through my heart**." (From Behind Palace Doors by Nigel Dempster and Peter Evans, 1993.)

## ARROW

– **as straight as an arrow** – pfeilgerade, wie an einer Schnur gezogen.

"The bullet shot through the air **as straight as an arrow** and scored a bull's eye." cf. as straight as a die; NB. *the idiom* **straight-arrow** *which is American English for an honest and law-abiding person.*

## A SUIT OF ARMOUR

– **like a suit of armour** – wie eine Ritterrüstung.

Throughout the flak, Wogan preserved his genial Irish charm, wrapping it around him **like a suit of armour**. (Lester Middlehurst writing about the TV star, Terry Wogan, Daily Mail, 15.4.1994.)

I think what saved me was having a thick skin – **it's like having a suit of armour**. (Daily Mail writing about Julia Outing's determination to get a house built for herself and her family, 7.7.1994.)

# 22. Tools – *Werkzeug*

## PIN

– **as neat/clean as a new pin** – sauber und ordentlich, aufgeräumt/ blitzsauber/wie aus dem Ei gepellt.

“After two hours’ hard work, the kitchen was **as neat as a new pin**.” cf. as clean as a whistle.

## NAIL

– **as hard/tough as nails** – hart wie Stein, gefühllos.

“Don’t bother to tell him about your dog’s illness. He’s **as hard as nails** and won’t comfort you.” cf. as hard as the nether millstone.

– **as dead as a door-nail/as dead as the nail in a coffin/as dead as a tent-peg** – mausetot. *It can apply to causes and campaigns, as well as people.*

“The campaign for spelling reform is **as dead as a door-nail**.”

Old Marley was **as dead as a door-nail**. Mind! I don’t mean to say that I know, of my own knowledge, what there is particularly dead about a door-nail. I might have been inclined, myself, to regard a coffin-nail as the deadest piece of ironmongery in the trade. (A Christmas Carol by Charles Dickens, 1843.)

cf. as dead as the dodo, stone-dead.

– **like a nail/like another nail in the coffin** – wie ein weiterer Nagel zu jemandes Sarg.

Clearly Princess Diana had no choice other than to take this decision, but her withdrawal from public life will be **like a nail in the coffin** of our monarchy. The rest of the Royals have just 10 per cent of her charisma and her decision has done no favours to Charles. (G.E. Pilgrim, Broxbourne. Daily Mail, 9.12.1993.)

## VICE

– **in a vice-like grip/ a grip like a vice** – wie ein Schraubstock.

The dog held the girl's arm **in a vice-like grip**.

The drug baron and his gang of drug pushers held the town **in a vice-like grip**.

Bonding with baby, in 1994, means wearing a dress that is often so small and so tight that it constrains Junior to your body **in a vice-like grip**. (Jane Gordon, Daily Mail, 26.7.1994.)

Simon remembered the stern face and **vice-like lips** of Madame Arnaud. (Hotel Pastis by Peter Mayle, 1993.)

## SLEDGE-HAMMER

– **one's heart is thumping like a sledge-hammer** – jemandes Herz schlägt wie ein Schmiedehammer/Rammbock/Dampfhammer/bis zum Hals.

When the lift suddenly got stuck, Sarah's **heart began to thump like a sledge-hammer**. cf. one's heart is beating like a drum.

– **pain/smell hits someone like a sledge-hammer** – Schmerz/Geruch trifft jemand wie ein Dampfhammer/ein Schlag.

"The plant I was carrying was too heavy and suddenly a pain in my back **hit me like a sledge-hammer**."

"The musty **stench** of this ghastly edifice **hit me like a sledge-hammer**." (Felidae by Akif Pirincii, 1989.)

## SPANNER

– **a face like a bag of spanners** – ein langweiliges, unattraktives Gesicht.

A brief glance at history shows that having **a face like a bag of spanners** does not necessarily prevent you having a whacking lot of fun and as many lovers as you please. (Jane Kelly, Daily Mail, 21.9.1993.) cf. a face as long as a fiddle; a face like thunder; to set one's face like flint.

## RAKE

– **as thin/lean as a rake** – schlank wie eine Gerte; dünn wie ein Strich; gertenschlank; spindeldürr.

After wandering around on the moor for six days the explorer was **as thin as a rake**. cf. to look like a string bean; as thin as a yard of pump water; drainpipe-thin; stick-thin; to look like a stick insect.

## POKER

– **to sit as stiff as a poker** – dasitzen, als ob man einen Besenstiel verschluckt hätte.

When her boyfriend did not turn up at the restaurant, Patricia **sat as stiff as a poker,** looking at the menu and wondering what to do next. c.f. as stiff as a ramrod/rod. *A variation:* **as stiff as a board**.

like putty/clay in s.o.'s hands

### PUTTY

– **as soft as putty, like putty/clay in someone's hands** – wie Wachs in jemandes Hand.

"If you give her a box of chocolates, she'll be **like putty in your hands**."

The wealthy banker was **like clay in the hands of** his sexy young secretary.

### SANDPAPER

– **skin/voice like sandpaper** – Haut/Stimme wie Schmirgelpapier.

Simon rubbed his unshaven face, and it **felt like frozen sandpaper**. (Hotel Pastis by Peter Mayle, 1993.)

"Don't talk", said Susie, "I can't make out what you're saying, anyway. You **sound like sandpaper** fighting a nutmeg grater." (King of Camberwell by Mary Jane Staples, 1990.)

## 23. Books and Stationery – *Bücher und Schreibwaren*

### LIBRARY

– **as quiet as a library** – still wie in einer Kirche; still wie der See; wie die Ruhe nach einem Sturm; mucksmäuschenstill.

After the departure of the politicians, journalists and photographers, the hotel was **as quiet as a library**. cf. as quiet as a mouse.

### ABC

– **as easy/simple as ABC** – ganz einfach, kinderleicht.

"It's a beautiful washing-machine and very modern. You'll find it's **as easy as ABC** to use." cf. as easy as pie; as easy as shelling peas;

as easy as slicing bread; as easy as falling off a log, as easy as winking; *and the opposite:* as easy as juggling with soot; as easy as nailing jelly to the wall.

## BOOK

– **like an open book/as open as a book/open as books** – wie ein offenes/aufgeschlagenes Buch.

"I needed closeness, honesty. My Mum always says to me: "You talk too openly." **I am like an open book, they're like clams**." (Claire Austin, a surrogate mother, Daily Mail, 26. 10. 1993.) cf. as open as the day; *and the opposite:* to close up like a clam, as close as an oyster.

– **to read someone like a book** – jemandes Gedanken lesen können; jemanden durchschauen.

"Whenever my nephew visits me, it is always to ask for money. No matter how carefully he leads up to the subject, **I can read him like a book**."

I can read him like a book.

## DICTIONARY/ENCYCLOPAEDIA

– **to talk/to be like a walking dictionary/encyclopaedia** – reden/gebildet sein wie ein wandelndes Lexikon.

"You can go and ask Paul to help you with your crossword puzzle. He's **like a walking dictionary**."

On rejecting The Shrieking Skeleton by Erle Stanley Gardner, 1937: The characters **talk like dictionaries** ... (From Rotten Rejections, The Letters That Publishers Wish They'd Never Sent. Edited by Andre Bernard, 1990.)

The terrorist, Carlos, is **like a walking encyclopaedia**, not only of the acts of terrorism that he was responsible for, but for everything that has occurred in that area for the last 25 years. (British author David Yallop who met Carlos five years ago while researching a book on him. Daily Mail, 16.8.1994.)

## WORD

– **to be as good as one's word** – sein Wort halten; zu seinem Wort stehen. *Often said when the promise is unlikely to be kept.*

"I never thought Pamela would keep her promise but she was **as good as her word**." (The Penguin Dictionary of English Idioms.)

## BOND

– **My word is as good as my bond** – mein Wort ist so gut wie meine Unterschrift; zu seinem Wort stehen.

"You can rely on my promise, even though it is not in writing. **My word is as good as my bond**." *Bond is a written agreement or pledge.* (The Penguin Dictionary of English Idioms.)

## CLICHÉ

– **to sound like a cliché** – abgedroschen/wie ein Klischee klingen.

"We get on well and although it may **sound like a cliché**, we're more like best friends than mother and daughter." (Penny Vincenzi, Daily Mail, 21.9.1993.)

Dying of a broken heart **sounds like a sentimental cliché** from some 19th century romantic novel, but some doctors and counsellors think it is a 20th century reality. (Lucy Hawking, Daily Mail, 14.6.1994.)

## CONFETTI

– **like confetti** – wie Heu/Konfetti.

"The local council has no financial worries because the taxpayers' money is pouring in **like confetti**."

## PAPER/PAPYRUS

– **as white as paper/papyrus** – käseweiß; kreidebleich; schneeweiß.

The dancer wore a long evening dress with a low neckline, displaying a décolleté **as white as papyrus**.

"The boy's back had never been exposed to the sun and it was **as white as paper**." cf. as white as snow/milk/a lily/sheet.

– **paper-thin** – dünn wie Papier; hauchdünn.

Whyever have these flats got such **paper-thin** walls? I can hear my neighbour practising on his piano and it is driving me mad.

Tom's Japanese friend offered him a helping of **paper-thin** seaweed squares.

## CARDBOARD

– **to taste like cardboard** – wie Hund/fürchterlich schmecken.

"I really can't eat this food. It **tastes just like cardboard**!"

## INK

– **as serene/still as ink** – ruhig und gelassen, gleichförmig wie ein Uhrwerk/eine Nähmaschine

The lovers drove off into the starlit night, their car purring **as serene as ink.** NB. inky stillness.

## GLUE

– **to stick to someone/something like glue** – wie eine Klette an jemandem hängen.

Silly me! I should have washed this pot straightaway but now the porridge is **sticking to it like glue**.

There are now roughly 400,000 nannies working in Britain. Once you have found your Spandex-clad Mary Poppins, **stick to her like glue**. (Kate Saunders, The Sunday Times, 12.9.1993.)

cf. to cling to someone like a limpet; to follow someone like a shadow.

## WAX

– **as close as wax** – verschwiegen/verschlossen wie ein Grab.

"The cook will never tell you what really happened. She is **as close as wax**." cf. as close as an oyster; as close as the grave; to shut up like a clam.

## RULER

– **as straight as a ruler** – kerzengerade; wie mit dem Lineal gezogen.

The road was **as straight as a ruler** and went on for miles.

The hairdresser had cut Claire's hair **as straight as a ruler**.

cf. as straight as a candle.

## 24. Stories – *Geschichten*

### PLAY

– **as good as a play/like a play** – wie im Kino/Film/Theater.

It was fascinating to see how the cunning lawyer managed to prove that the boxing champion had not really killed his wife – it was **as good as a play**.

"The Queen said the whole of the Coronation was **like a play**." Spoken by Historic Royal Palaces curator Simon Thurley, (Daily Mail, 25.3.1994.)

### FAIRY-TALE

– **to be/sound/read/look like a fairy-tale** – wie in einem Märchen, märchenhaft sein/klingen/sich lesen/aussehen.

It **was like a fairy-tale**, but unlike most fairy-stories the happy ending came at the beginning. Almost everywhere Communism collapsed swiftly and with little bloodshed. (Mark Almond, Daily Mail, 21.9.1993.)

Marion was dressed so prettily for the party that she **looked** just **like a fairy-tale princess**.

### DREAM

– **to work like a dream** – funktionieren wie im Traum/traumhaft/wunderbar klappen wie am Schnürchen.

The enemy – Council workmen sent to build a site for travellers – was repulsed and peace returned temporarily to the Somerset backwater. The operation to guard the site entrance 24 hours a day, summoning help when the workmen arrive, has **worked like a dream**. (Chris Brooke, Daily Mail, 26.6.1993.) cf. worked like magic.

– **to fit like a dream** – passen wie im/ein Traum, traumhaft/wunderbar/wie angegossen passen.

I love this dress! It's so glamorous and sophisticated and it **fits me like a dream**.

– **to write like a dream** – traumhaft/wunderbar schreiben.

No wonder that best-selling author got so famous. He **writes like a dream**. cf. to write like an angel.

– **to go like a dream/like a charm** – laufen wie geschmiert/wie eine Eins. *The phrase is usually applied to cars, yachts or aeroplanes.*

Today was the first time that I drove my new car and it **went like a dream**. cf. go like a bird.

– **It was like a dream/dream-like/like a dream come true** – es war traumhaft/wie ein Traum(, der wahr wird.)

These months with you are different, like nothing that's ever happened before. **It's been like a dream**, stolen out of time. (The Shell Seekers by Rosamunde Pilcher, 1987.)

"We are trying to recreate the **dream-like** state hypnotherapists can induce." Steve Henry of the advertising agency HHCL which produced the first TV commercial using a hypnotist. (Daily Mail, 2.12.1994. *This commercial was dropped.*)

"I sat at some big star's feet and read one line. But **being in film at all was like a dream come true to me**: it seemed the pinnacle of my childhood ambition. (The film star Shirley Anne Field. Daily Mail, 1.7.1993.)

– **to sound like a pipe dream** – wie ein frommer Wunsch/Wunschtraum klingen.

Bernard Lavery's dearest ambition is to persuade aid agencies in the Third World to take out seeds of his giant vegetables to help the starving. "It might **sound like a bit of a pipe dream**, but it would make my life's work worthwhile if they took me up on it," he says. "Just think how many people could have a good meal from a 108 lb. 2 oz marrow." (Tim Walker, Daily Mail, 30.9.1993.) NB. *the idiom:* pie in the sky.

– **like a bad dream** – wie ein Alptraum.

It was **like a bad dream** when the writer realised she had mistakenly erased a whole chapter of her new book on the computer.

– **like a nightmare/like a nightmare come true** – wie in einem Alptraum/der wahr wird.

**It was like a nightmare** when we discovered that our car had been stolen, together with our suitcases and passports.

– **to vanish like a dream** – wie vom Erdboden verschwinden.

When little Vladek came to live in Germany he had to learn German and soon all his Polish **vanished like a dream**. cf. to disappear like water on sand. *Variations:* **to vanish like a pricked balloon; to vanish like smoke.**

## GIANT

– **as tall as a giant** – riesengroß, riesig.

"Have you seen the new basketball player yet? He's **as tall as a giant**!"

## DRAGON

– **as fierce as a dragon** – wild und grimmig; ein alter Drachen.

I'm rather afraid of our new Maths teacher. She's **as fierce as a dragon**.

– **as common as dragon's teeth** – sehr ungewöhnlich/selten; so selten wie ein Sechser im Lotto.

In this part of the country, where men have always been men, homosexuals are about **as common as dragons' teeth**. (Mason Willey, Nottinghamshire, Daily Mail, 27.1.1994.) cf. like hen's teeth; as common as comets.

She's as fierce as a dragon.

## JANUS

– **Janus-like** – wie ein Januskopf, januskopfig.

Science is represented in the media as two-faced, **Janus-like**. On the one hand there is technological gee-whizzery and on the other are the mad scientists, the mad Frankensteins. (The Making of Memory by Steven Rose, 1992.)

## METHUSELAH

– **as old as Methuselah** – alt wie Methusalem, steinalt, uralt.

That joke is **as old as Methuselah**.

The English teacher was **as old as Methuselah.** He had been teaching at the school for sixty years. *Methuselah is a mythical figure who was reputed to have lived for 969 years.* cf. as old as Adam.

## DAMOCLES

– **like the sword of Damocles hanging over one** – als ob ein Damoklesschwert über einem hängt.

"It had been **like living with the sword of Damocles hanging over my head**. I can't describe the terror, knowing the odds were so terrific. Cancer has caused so much grief and destruction in my family that the surgery to remove my breasts was an emotional and psychological relief." (Charlynn Ross, Daily Mail, 30.11.1993.)

*A variation:* **to hang like a hammer over someone's head.** cf. like a cloud/a dark cloud/a poison cloud.

## PANDORA

– **like Pandora's box** – wie die Büchse der Pandora.

The astrologer, Jonathan Cainer, wishes to investigate the dark side of your moon and help you explore your dreams and feelings: "It may be **like opening up a Pandora's box**, for the moon has much to do with the irrational, intuitive side of your nature." (Daily Mail, 6.12.1994.)

At the Antiquarian Book Fair in Bloomsbury, London, one gets a tingling sensation from opening a volume that may have remained closed for 100 years. A book that has kept it's mouth shut until one opens it, **like Pandora's box**, to let out the words, free the memory. (A. A. Gill, Style and Travel, The Sunday Times, 3. 7. 1994.) NB. *the American idiom warning one to leave an ugly can of worms tightly shut.*

## SPHINX

– **like a sphinx/sphinx-like** – undurchschaubar/mysteriös wie eine Sphinx.

"Have you seen the leader of the Pantheist Society yet? She looks so beautiful and **sphinx-like** – I must get to know her!"

## HAMLET

– **like Hamlet without the Prince** – *etwa*: als ob die Hauptfigur fehlt; wie ein Fisch ohne Wasser.

"To have the last day of the party conference without the leader would be **like Hamlet without the Prince**."

"A king needs a consort. A monarchy without a queen is **like Hamlet without a Prince**." (Mary Kenny writing about Prince Charles, Daily Mail, 30. 6. 1994.) cf. like bread without butter.

– **Hamlet-like indecision** – hoffnungslos unentschlossen.

Charles was desperately trying to extricate himself from the forthcoming marriage to Lady Diana ... There was another reason why the Prince's **Hamlet-like indecision** was being ignored by those who knew him. "Being beset and vacillating is simply Charles's way," said a courtier smugly. "Nothing is so sure to me as his uncertainty." (Behind Palace Doors by Nigel Dempster and Peter Evans, 1993.)

## ALADDIN's CAVE

– **like an Aladdin's cave** – wie in Aladins Höhle.

I love shopping for fabrics. I go to Southall where they have marvellous stuff. There's one shop with the best fabrics from the whole of India all under one roof, **like an Aladdin's cave**. (Sandy Powell, a costume designer for dance and films. Sunday Times, 4. 7. 1993.)

## PUNCH

– **to be as pleased as Punch** – mit sich im höchsten Maße zufrieden sein, sich wie ein Schneekönig freuen.

"My son is **as pleased as Punch**. He got the best mark for spelling in his class."

## ALICE IN WONDERLAND

– **like Alice in Wonderland/Alice-like** – widersprüchlich; unverständlich; unlogisch.

"First, I am blamed for locking the door, then the next day, I am blamed for not locking it. It's **like Alice in Wonderland**."

"But with his triumph in persuading Congress to pass the American free trade agreement, Bill Clinton demonstrated that he can be tough and ruthless in his determination to get what he wants. It was just **like an Alice in Wonderland situation** when the Yes vote came in – the president's most fervent supporters were the opposition Republicans, while his most bitter opponents were Democrats, prominent members of his own party." (Tony Burton, Daily Mail, 19.11.1993.)

It is the essence of bureaucracy to manipulate the language so that, **Alice-like**, a word can mean anything one chooses, without reference to the dictionary. (Keith Waterhouse, Daily Mail, 2.12.1993.)

## CHESHIRE CAT

– **to grin/smile like a Cheshire Cat** – 1. grinsen wie ein Honigkuchenpferd, 2. etwas, das nur sichtbar wird, wenn man bewußt danach sucht, 3. nur der substanzlose Schein bleibt.

The chemistry teacher **grinned like a Cheshire Cat** whilst he was handing out the examination papers.

"The red-light district in Amsterdam is a fairly safe place to visit. No soliciting in the streets, no kerb crawling. The red-light district is **like the Cheshire Cat's smile:** it is invisible unless you know where to look for it. You can live all your life in Amsterdam without ever setting foot there, or even getting an inkling of its existence." (Vitali Vitaliev, The European, 25.2.1993.)

"Britain has come increasingly to rely upon the charm of her diplomats and politicians to draw attention away from, and shore up, her declining strength. British power has slowly disappeared, leaving, **like the Cheshire Cat**, only a wide smile behind." (Andrew Roberts, Daily Mail, 1994.) *The English county of Cheshire is famous for its cheese and might at one time have had the head of a grinning cat stamped on them.*

## MARY POPPINS

– **to make something look like Mary Poppins** – etwas vergleichsweise sehr harmlos/wie einen Spaziergang erscheinen lassen.

Charles Saatchi's advertisements make previous campaigns **look like Mary Poppins**. (The Sunday Times, 21.8.1988.) cf. like a vicarage tea-party. *Variations:* **like a picnic; to look like a Bobbsey Twins escapade**.

## TOPSY

– **to be/grow like Topsy/like Topsy – it just grew/it just growed** – sich von selbst entwickeln. *'growed' is the original expression and is still used today, although one can also say 'grew' and 'has grown'.*

The Milton Keynes dialect appeared so suddenly, and **like Topsy has grown**, so that now everyone has heard of it.

## JURASSIC PARK

– **in a Jurassic-Park-like manner** – altmodisch, wie die Dinosaurier.

Chinese Russians are unique, since, in **a Jurassic-Park-like manner,** they carry the old Russian culture. It was a culture destroyed by the Bolsheviks, and is no longer to be found in Russia. (Vitali Vitaliev, The European, 19.11.1993.)

The more dramatic the battle to defeat the **Jurassic Park Socialists** who want to retain Clause Four, the more powerful Mr Blair's appeal to the electorate. (Comment, Daily Mail, 12.1.1995.)

## 25. People – *Menschen*

### CELEBRITY

– **to treat someone like a celebrity** – jemanden wie einen Prominenten/VIP/eine Respektsperson feiern/behandeln.

After bringing all the hostages safely back home, the priest was **treated like a celebrity.**

### DWARF

– **to feel like a dwarf next to someone** – sich wie ein Zwerg/Winzling/unscheinbar neben jemandem fühlen.

"Standing beside me was a young man who must have been at least two meters tall. I **felt like a dwarf** next to him."

I felt like a dwarf next to him.

## HERMIT

– **to live like a hermit/hermit-like** – (abgeschieden und zurückgezogen leben) wie ein Eremit/Einsiedler.

The prince's behaviour in the first months of their marriage was indeed selfish and peculiar: sitting, in his words, "**hermit-like**" during their honeymoon on the royal yacht Britannia, reading van der Post on Jung, while Diana "dashes about chatting up all the sailors". (The Prince of Wales, A Biography by Jonathan Dimbleby, 1994.)

Whitney Houston begins the British leg of a marathon world tour in Birmingham in a fortnight. She is reported to have become **like a hermit** on the road, resting through the day and rarely seeing visitors. (Baz Bamigboye, Daily Mail, 15.10.1993.)

## MONK

– **a monk-like cell** – wie die Zelle eines Mönches/Mönchszelle.

The overweight business manager was given **a monk-like cell** on the health farm.

## WAIF

– **waif-like** – *etwa:* Beschützerinstinkte/Barmherzigkeit erwekkend wie ein heimatloses Kind.

Kate Moss would hate women who actually look like women with hips, busts and curves in all the right places. You know Kate Moss ... **drainpipe-thin**, with a boy's face and a **waif-like** ambience that makes you want to put her into care. (Annabelle Forsyth, The Mail on Sunday, 14.8.1994.)

Most women can only dream of a figure like hers (a perfect size 12 measuring 36-24-35). Yet to a fashion industry obsessed with **waif-like** women, Claire Pearton is classed as an outsize model. (Tracy Harrison, Daily Mail, 26.7.1994.) cf. the adjective: waif-faced.

## MISER

– **like a miser** – wie ein Geizhals/Geizkragen.

"And who opened the account?" Zaugg hesitated. He was **like a miser** with his store of precious information: parting with each fact was agony. (Fatherland by Robert Harris, 1992.)

## THIEF

– **to steal away like a thief in the night** – sich davonstehlen wie ein Dieb in der Nacht.

The dampness and fogs of the past week **had stolen away like thieves into the night**. (From The Woman in Black by Susan Hill, 1983.)

– **to be as thick as thieves** – durch Pech und Schwefel miteinander gehen; dicke Freunde sein.

"Those two won't tell me anything about the wedding plans. They are **as thick as thieves** and I'm so curious."

## CRIMINAL

– **to feel/treat like a criminal** – sich wie ein Krimineller fühlen/ wie einen Kriminellen behandeln.

On leaving the shop, a store detective demanded to search my bag in front of many onlookers. **I felt like a criminal**.

"Don't **treat me like a criminal**, because I am innocent." (Michael Jackson, Daily Mail, 23.12.1993.)

## PARIAH

– **to treat someone as a pariah** – jemanden wie einen Aussätzigen behandeln.

I want the air in my restaurant to stay clean and fresh and all smokers shall be **treated as pariahs.** cf. treat like a leper/like dirt/like a toe-rag/like animals/like a dog/whipped dogs. *A pariah is an outcast. Originally a member of a low caste of S. India and Burma.*

## FOOL

– **like a fool/like the fool he/she was** – wie ein Idiot/Dummkopf/ dumm wie er/sie war.

"And Peter, **like the fool he was**, went right up to my ex-boyfriend and asked him if he still loved me!"

When Pamela saw an old friend singing and dancing at a bus stop she asked him: "Why are you **behaving like a fool**?"

cf. lived like a man and died like a dog; it is better to die like a hero than live like a worm.

## IDIOT

– **like an idiot/to look like a complete idiot** – wie ein Trottel/ Idiot/wie ein vollkommener Idiot aussehen.

On going into the restaurant, my coat button got tangled up with a plant decoration, and there I stood **like a complete idiot** in full view of everyone clutching the whole plant in my hands.

## TWERP

– **to feel like a twerp/a right twerp** – sich blöd vorkommen.

"I **felt like a right twerp** when all the snow fell off the roof on top of me!" *Twerp is a silly fool. 'twerp' was created from the name of a student at Oxford in the early 20th century called T. W. Earp. He was well-known for his foolish behaviour.*

## ZOMBIE

– **like a zombie/zombie-like/zombie-like state** – wie ein Zombie/Roboter/eine Marionette/roboterhaft; wie im Tran.

"One police statement describes River Phoenix as being **like a zombie**. His arms and legs moved in jerking motions. His eyes were glazed." (George Gordon, Daily Mail, 6.11.1993 describing the fatal effects of drugs on this famous actor.)

My hot bubble bath and the delicious fruit punch relaxed me to an almost **zombie-like state**.

## FRUMP

– **to look like a frump** – wie eine Vogelscheuche aussehen *(only of a woman).*

"I realised I was getting to **look like a frump**. So I changed my eating habits. I think you can look better than you really are if you smile a lot." (Actress Sue Pollard, Daily Mail, 7.1.1995.)

## BIMBO

– **to treat someone like a bimbo** – eine hübsche Frau wie ein dümmliches Sexualobjekt behandeln.

In the City, men behave like wolves hunting in a pack and feeding off each other. If one **treats you like a bimbo**, the others will. (Samantha Phillips, a victim of sexual discrimination, talking about life as a woman in the male-dominated City of London, Daily Mail, 14.8.1994.)

## TRAMP

– **to look like a tramp** – wie ein Landstreicher/Vagabund aussehen.

Favell **looked like a tramp**, his trousers were old, the soles of his shoes were flapping open. His collar was greasy, his hair uncut, unwashed. (Mrs de Winter by Susan Hill, 1993.) cf. to look like a scarecrow; to look like one has been dragged through a hedge backwards; to look like nothing on earth; to look like the wreck of Hesperus; to look like a bag lady.

# 26. Work and Occupations – *Arbeit und Beruf*

## CINCH

– **to sound like a cinch** – kinderleicht klingen.

“Writing about women who wear haute couture **sounded like a cinch**. How hard could it be to find a few glamorous women willing to talk about their clothes? But astonishingly, not one of the 25 women I contacted – all known for wearing beautiful, custom-made clothes – would agree to discuss the presumably exciting process of purchasing a couture dress.” (Cosima von Bulow, Daily Mail, 4.11.1993.) *A cinch is a task performed with ease.*

## BUSINESS

– **like nobody’s business** – wie verrückt; sehr intensiv.

Most of the people in the doctor’s waiting-room were coughing and sneezing **like nobody’s business**.

– **business-like/in a business-like way/manner,** etc. – geschäftsmäßig.

I know that we have been friends for a very long time, but if you want to rent my house we must be **business-like** and make a proper contract.

## JUDGE

– **as sober as a judge** – stocknüchtern; betont sachlich; nüchtern, trocken und ungerührt.

“Pickled? I’m **as sober as a judge**.” Retired judge James Pickles, brought in to spice up GMTV’s ritual look at the morning papers, was dramatically taken off the air yesterday after seven minutes of chaos. (Bill Mouland, Daily Mail, 18.10.1993.) *Pickled is slang for drunk.*

Everyone else was laughing and joking but he was **as sober as a judge**.

## DOCTOR

– **as tactful as a doctor** – taktvoll und diskret wie ein Diplomat.

The bank manager talked kindly to the young married couple and was **as tactful as a doctor**.

## STEEPLEJACK

– **to climb like a steeplejack** – klettern wie ein Affe.

"You should have seen him up on that mountain. He **climbs like a steeplejack**." cf. to climb like a monkey.

## BUMMAREE

– **to swear like a bummaree** – fluchen wie ein Bierkutscher/Landsknecht.

There seems to be general agreement that John Major has done himself no end of good by **swearing like a bummaree** on that bootlegged video tape. (Keith Waterhouse, Daily Mail, 29.7.1993.) *A Bummaree is a middleman at Billingsgate fish-market.* cf. to swear like a trooper. *A variation:* **to swear like an ostler.**

## NAVVY

– **hands like a navvy's** – Hände wie ein Landarbeiter/Bauer/Straßenarbeiter/Bauarbeiter.

Susan looked at her hands in dismay. "I'll never be ready for the party in time. After all that gardening, **my hands are like a navvy's**."

## SLAVE

– **to work like a slave** – wie ein Pferd/Kuli arbeiten.

"Don't go there as a maid, Charlotte. They'll make you **work like a slave** in that house!" cf. to work like a Trojan/like a dog/like a horse/like hell. *A variation:* **work like a navvy**.

## DUMMY

– **like a tailor's dummy** – wie ein Geck/Modenarr/Dandy.

"Can you see that young man in the purple suit over there? He **looks like a tailor's dummy**." *Variation:* **to dress like a dandy.**

## SANDBOY

– **as happy as a sandboy** – kreuzfidel/quietschfidel/sehr glücklich und ausgelassen.

Juliane Christiansen, Isaiah's mother, is a strong endorsement for the curative powers of alcohol. When she's sober, she is stiff, mute, and inhibited. When she's drunk, she is lively and **happy as a sandboy**. (Miss Smilla's Feeling For Snow by Peter Hoeg, 1992.) cf. as happy as Larry/as a lark/as a dog with two tails/as a pig in horseshit/as the day is long.

as happy as a sandboy

# 27. Money and Valuables – *Geld und Wertsachen*

## MONEY

– **to spend money like water/like it's going out of fashion** – Geld rinnt einem durch die Hände wie Wasser; Geld zum Fenster hinauswerfen.

"Just look at all those shopping bags! You are **spending our money like water**." NB. *the idiom:* money down the drain.

– **like taking money from blind beggars** – als ob man einem Blinden in die Tasche greift/die Almosen stiehlt.

"How dare they do that to those poor investors! It's **like taking money from blind beggars**."

## COIN

– **to be like twin faces of a coin** – wie zwei Seiten einer Medaille sein.

They are **like twin faces of a coin** – irredeemably linked. On one side the Prince and Princess of Wales. On the other Andrew and Camilla Parker Bowles. (Richard Kay, Daily Mail, 24.10.1994.)

Life and death are **like twin faces of a coin**.

## PENNY

– **to turn up like a bad penny** – *etwa:* immer wieder und zur Unzeit auftauchen.

Oh no! There's my former boyfriend again. He's always **turning up like a bad penny**.

## NINEPENCE

– **as right as ninepence** – munter wie ein Fisch im Wasser; kerngesund.

"Spend a few days in bed and you'll soon feel **as right as nine-pence** again." cf. as right as rain/as a trivet; as fit as a fiddle.

– **as nimble as ninepence** – gewandt wie ein Aal/eine Schlange/ein Mensch ohne Knochen.

Jo's father had lost the front door key so he had to be **as nimble as ninepence** and climb in through the kitchen window. cf. *the opposite:* as nimble as a cow in a cage/as an eel in a sandbag.

## CENT

– **to feel like two cents** – sich schämen; verlegen sein. *An American simile.*

The father scolded his daughter for being clumsy with the milk, but when he spilt his tea a few moments later he **felt like two cents**.

## DOLLAR

– **to feel/look like a million dollars** – sich fabelhaft/pudelwohl/ausgesprochen attraktiv fühlen.

"Christina Onassis was even happier after having an operation in Paris to re-shape the hawk nose she had inherited from Ari and to remove the dark circles under her eyes. She **felt like a million dollars**, she said." (The Story of Christina Onassis by Nigel Dempster, 1989.)

After having saved the dog's life, the vet **felt like a million dollars**.

– **as sound as a dollar** – zuverlässig wie die Deutsche Bundesbahn; ausgesprochen zuverlässig.

"This vacuum cleaner has been on the market for many years and you may rest assured that it is **as sound as a dollar"**, the shop assistant told his customer. *The United States dollar was considered to be the most stable currency in the world.*

## PURSE

– **like having a purse with a hole** – als ob man ein Loch in der Geldbörse hat.

like having a purse with a hole

Playing Polo at about £ 33,000 a year is **like having a purse with a hole**.

## CHEQUE

– **like handing someone a blank cheque** – als ob man jemandem einen Blankoscheck ausstellt.

As for Japanese trees, putting one of these in your front garden is **like handing the shrub bandits a blank cheque**. (Chris Middleton investigating garden thieves. Daily Mail Weekend, 23.7.1994.)

## DEBT

– **to hang over someone like an overdue debt** – wie eine dunkle Wolke/ein dunkler Schatten über jemanden hängen.

Drought in the Luberon **hangs over the farmers like an overdue debt**. (Toujours Provence by Peter Mayle, 1991.) cf. to hang over someone like a dark cloud/a poison cloud.

## GOLD

– **as good as gold** – brav wie ein Engel.

The nanny told the proud parents that their baby was **as good as gold**.

– **to shine like pure gold** – wie reines Gold glänzen.

Once upon a time there was a little girl who lived on the edge of a big wood. She had very beautiful **hair**, which hung in long curls down her back. In the rays of the sun it **shone like pure gold**, and so she was called Goldilocks. (Goldilocks And The Three Bears, Ladybird Books.)

– **like gold dust** – rar/selten/dünn gesät.

The Job Centre manager told Howard that jobs in this area are **like gold dust**. Now he is thinking of moving to London.

– **to treat something like gold** – etwas hüten wie seinen Augapfel/ nicht aus den Augen lassen.

When you are abroad, don't lose your passport. **Treat it like gold**.

– **like gold at the end of the rainbow** – etwas Unerreichbares/ein Wunschtraum/ein Wolkenkuckucksheim.

I've been inventing board games for five years now. I'd love to get one of them published but deep down I know **it's like gold at the end of the rainbow**.

## JEWEL

– **to shine/twinkle like a jewel** – glitzern wie ein Edelstein/Juwel.

The lake **shone like a jewel** in the early morning sunshine.

## GEM

– **like a rare gem** – wie ein seltener Edelstein; Spitzenklasse.

Caroline's essay on horses is **like a rare gem.** I'm sure she'll be a writer when she grows up.

## DIAMOND

– **like a diamond** – strahlend/glitzernd wie ein Diamant.

Twinkle, twinkle, little star,
How I wonder what you are!
Up above the world so high,
**Like a diamond** in the sky. *A nursery rhyme.*

– **as bright as a diamond/diamond-bright** – brillant, intelligent und schlagfertig.

The thriller writing is **diamond-bright**, as is the intuitive Miss Smilla. (Daily Mail Book Review of Miss Smilla's Feeling For Snow by Peter Hoeg, 25.11.1994.)

– **eyes sparkle/glisten like diamonds** – Augen, die wie Diamanten strahlen/glitzern.

Louisa told me about her engagement to the handsome film star and her **eyes sparkled like diamonds**.

Steffi Graf is a **dream-like** creation with **eyes that glisten like diamonds** and **hair like silk**. (Daily Mail, 13.10.1993.)

## RUBY

– **ruby-red** – rot wie ein Rubin, rubinrot

The advertisement showed us a pretty girl seductively kissing a chocolate with her **ruby-red** lips. cf. blood-red.

## EMERALD

– **emerald-green** – grün wie ein Smaragd, smaragdgrün.

The Irish pop singer was strikingly attractive with her long chestnut hair and **emerald-green** eyes.

### SAPPHIRE

– **sapphire-blue** – strahlend blau, saphierblau.

Mary's blue dress brought out the **sapphire-blue** colour of her eyes perfectly. *A variation:* **eyes as blue as forget-me-nots**.

### PEARL

– **pearl-white** – perlweiß.

On the toothpaste advertisement the model laughed merrily and showed us her **pearl-white** teeth. cf. milk-white.

### CHARITY

– **as cold as charity** – gefühlskalt; ohne innere Anteilnahme; kalt wie eine Hundeschnauze.

"Don't bother to ask your boss to sponsor your walk. He's **as cold as charity**." cf. as cold as marble; as cold as steel; as cold as ice; as cold as a paddock.

## 28. Toys and Games – *Spielzeug und Spiele*

### TOYS

– **to look like toys** – wie Spielzeuge aussehen.

It was a thrilling experience for us to sit high up in the sky in our air balloon. The houses and animals far below us **looked like toys**.

– **to treat something like a toy/like toys** – mit etwas umgehen, als sei es ein Spielzeug/etwas wie Spielzeug behandeln.

In England, children as young as seven and eight buy fireworks and **treat them like toys**, playing with them and lighting them.

Norman Lamont **treated** the Treasury **like a favourite toy** from which a spoilt child refuses to be parted. (Comment, Daily Mail, 10.6.1993.)

## DOLL

– **like a doll/like a little doll/as pretty as a doll** – wie eine Puppe/wie eine kleine Puppe/hübsch wie eine Puppe.

"Your baby is **as pretty as a doll**", the nurse told the proud young mother.

That little actress is so pretty. **She's just like a doll**.

– **as limp as a rag doll** – wie ein nasser Sack.

Alexandra sat contentedly next to her boy-friend in the discotheque, sipping her hot punch and feeling **as limp as a rag doll**.

– **as pale as a wax doll** – käsebleich, bleich wie der Tod.

The young couple found the little baby in an orphanage in Romania. He looked very sweet but was **as pale as a wax doll**.

– **a china-doll complexion** – Teint wie aus Porzellan.

The professional image-maker advised the television star on what to eat, how to dress and how to keep her **china-doll complexion**. cf. skin like porcelain.

## ROCKING-HORSE

– **to be as scarce as rocking-horse manure** – sehr selten/ungewöhnlich sein/Seltenheitswert haben.

"Houses with gardens in this part of town **are as scarce as rocking-horse manure**." *Of Australian origin.*

## DOMINOES

– **to spread like a game of dominoes** – sich in alle (vier) Winde verteilen.

The lawyer had only moved into his new office a week ago but now his documents had **spread like a game of dominoes** everywhere.

## YO-YO

– **to go/pop in and out like yo-yos/to bounce around like a yo-yo** – rein- und rauslaufen/hin- und herspringen wie ein Jo-Jo.

Powerful men such as Jack Jones of the Transport and General and Hugh Scanlon of the Engineers **were in and out** of Downing Street **like yo-yos** – so much so that Wilson was once prompted to tell Scanlon: "Keep your tanks off my lawn." (Daily Mail, 4. 11. 1992.)

My mischievous cousin, Stephen, **popped in and out** of my childhood **like a yo-yo**.

"My teenage son is so moody at the moment", Mrs Martin complained. "He is either very lethargic or he's **bouncing around like a yo-yo**!"

– **to diet like a yo-yo/yo-yo dieting** – Schlankheitskuren machen/abnehmen mit Jo-Jo-Effekt, abnehmen und gleich wieder zunehmen.

The Carbohydrate Addict's Diet, another American import, is the lifelong solution to **yo-yo dieting**, claim the diet's creators, Drs Rachael and Richard Heller. (Daily Mail, 26. 8. 1994.) *Yo-yo eating is the constant cycle of crash dieting followed by weight gain.*

## MAGIC

– **like magic/to work like magic** – wie (durch) ein Wunder/Wunder wirken.

"Your honey and onion drink **worked like magic**. My cough has completely gone!"

However did you manage to get that terrible stain out of my carpet? It has completely gone – **just like magic**! cf. work like a dream/like hell/like a dog/horse/beavers/like hell/like a Trojan/a slave/a navvy.

## KITE

– **to feel as high as a kite** – 1. sich wie im siebenten Himmel fühlen. 2. "high" sein, unter Drogen stehen.

Walking barefoot across the meadow, hand in hand with her boyfriend, Melissa felt **as high as a kite**.

The drug addict sat on the partly demolished wall, surrounded by tramps and drunks, and **as high as a kite**.

## GAME

– **like a game** – wie ein sportlicher Wettkampf, wie ein Spiel.

Yet court proceedings have become far too much **like a game**. The objective should be to get at the truth, but far too often rituals and technicalities get in the way. (Thames Valley chief constable Charles Pollard, Daily Mail, 18.9.1993.)

## DARTS

– **a dart-like nose** – eine spitze Nase.

Despite Concorde's age, its streamlined good looks, **dart-like nose**, delta wings and awesome power make onlookers gaze up in amazement when one passes overhead.

## NINEPINS

– **to fall for someone like ninepins** – jemandem verfallen/zu Füßen liegen.

The film star was so beautiful and charming that men **fell for her like ninepins**. cf. to fall like flies.

## BILLIARD

– **to be as bald as a billiard ball** – eine spiegelblanke Glatze haben/vollkommen glatzköpfig sein.

"The pop star shaved off all his hair. Now he is **as bald as a billiard ball**." cf. as bald as a coot; as bald as a bandicoot.

Men fell for her like ninepins.

## GOLF

– **eyes look like golf balls** – große Augen machen/die Augen aufreißen.

When the little girl saw that the ceiling of the grotto was covered in sea-shells, **her eyes looked like golf balls**. cf. eyes as big as saucers/plates.

## BALLOON

– **to swell like a balloon** – anschwellen/sich aufblähen wie ein Luftballon.

"If you eat too many peas and onions," the doctor said to his patient, "your stomach will **swell like a balloon**."

– **to go down like a lead balloon/to go over like a lead balloon** – einschlagen wie eine Bombe.

Alan's decision to leave school shortly before taking his final exams and to become a pop singer **went down like a lead balloon** with his parents. cf. words fall like lead.

The plan to build the new railway line through the park **went over like a lead balloon**. *An American simile.*

## SQUIB

– **to sputter like a damp squib** – verpuffen, im Sande verlaufen, ein Reinfall sein.

The campaign to paint all the lamp-posts in the town bright pink **sputtered like a damp squib** because the council ran out of money.

## ROCKET

– **to take off like a rocket** – einen kometenhaften Aufstieg nehmen.

Pamela's career as an actress **took off like a rocket** after she married the film director.

– **prices/shares shoot up like a rocket** – Preise/Aktien schnellen in die Höhe.

If only we had bought some more of those stamp sets. Now they have **shot up like a rocket.** cf. prices/rents go sky-high.

# 29. Music – *Musik*

## MUSIC

– **like music to one's ears** – Musik in jemandes Ohren sein/wie Musik in jemandes Ohren klingen.

"I heard that the secretary of the Cooking Society had to resign because she said you were too fat to become a member. That must have been **like music to your ears**, Nancy!"

## VIOLIN

– **as taut as a violin string** – unter Hochspannung/Hochdruck stehend; mit angespannten Nerven; verkrampft.

**Taut as a violin string** Penelope twanged and snapped, overdosing on pills, hitting the bottle, and falling into the beds of various captivating, if unreliable, arty types. Interestingly, at the time of her divorce she had published two novels to John's five but was the better known writer by far. (Val Hennessy reviewing About Time Too (1940–1978) by Penelope Mortimer, Daily Mail, 16. 10. 1993.)

– **one's nerves are twanging like violin strings** – jemandes Nerven sind zum Zerreißen gespannt.

Just before going onto the stage to sing in front of the royal audience, Amy's **nerves were twanging like violin strings**. cf. one's heart is beating like a drum.

## FIDDLE

– **as fit as a fiddle** – fit wie eine Eins/wie ein Turnschuh, topfit.

The army doctor thoroughly examined the young soldier and pronounced him **as fit as a fiddle.** cf. as fit as a flea; as sound as a bell; as right as rain; as right as a trivet.

as fit as a fiddle

– **guts as tight as fiddle strings** – wie unter Hochspannung stehend, die Nerven zum Zerreißen gespannt.

The reporter crouched down next to the soldiers in the besieged town, his **guts as tight as fiddle strings**.

– **as drunk as a fiddler** – voll wie eine Haubitze, sternhagelvoll.

By the time the old man left the pub, he was **as drunk as a fiddler**. cf. as drunk as a lord; as drunk as blazes.

– **to have a face like a fiddle/to have a face as long as a fiddle** – ein langes Gesicht machen.

"Jonathan's **face** was **as long as a fiddle** when he realised he had missed his favourite television programme." cf. a face like thunder; a face like flint.

## DRUM AND BRASS CYMBALS

– **one's heart beats like a drum/like brass cymbals** – das Herz schlägt einem bis zum Hals.

Natalie's **heart was beating like a drum** whilst the exam results were being read out. cf. one's heart is thumping like a sledge-hammer.

– **The sun beats on something like a drum** – die Sonne brennt vom Himmel herab/eine brütende Hitze liegt über etwas.

**The sun beats** on the Saudi Arabian desert **like a drum**.

– The **sun hits something/someone like a brass cymbal** – die Hitze trifft etwas/jemanden wie ein Keulenschlag.

"**The sun hit the crown of his head like a brass cymbal**. He had never known it so hot in May." (From The Darling Buds of May by H. E. Bates, 1958.)

– **to lock something up as tight as a drum** – etwas verriegeln und verrammeln.

No one will be able to steal my lawn-mower. The garden shed is **locked up as tight as a drum**.

The burglar was furious to find that the film star's house was **locked up tighter than a drum**.

– **as tight as a snare drum** – sehr geizig/ein Geizhals/Geizkragen.

"How stingy you are! Is that all you're going to give to charity? You're **as tight as a snare drum**!"

– **the wall is throbbing like a drumhead** – die Wände wackeln.

My neighbour had his radio on very loudly and **the wall** between us **was throbbing like a drumhead**.

– **rain sounds like the beating of drums** – der Regen trommelt auf ...

We found shelter from the storm in a little hut. The pounding **rain** on the roof **sounded like the beating of drums**.

## WHISTLE

– **as clean as a whistle** – 1. blitzblank 2. sauber, clean 3. perfekt.

The housewife scrubbed the frying-pan until it was **as clean as a whistle**.

The acrobat dived through the ring of fire **clean as a whistle**.

The policeman searched the young man's bag but it was **as clean as a whistle**.

"My son is **as clean as a whistle**, I promise you, Inspector. He would never take drugs." cf. as clean as a new pin.

*And last but not least:*

## NOTHING LIKE

– **there is nothing like** – es geht nichts über.

There is simply **nothing like** being curled up cosily in an armchair and reading a nice book ... or dictionary!

# Register

## A

## M



## N

**T**



**V**



**W**

**Y**



**Z**